BRIDGE WITH BRUNNER: ACOL BIDDING FOR IMPROVERS

by Michelle Brunner

B.T. Batsford Ltd, *London*

First published 2000

© Michelle Brunner 2000

ISBN 0 7134 8625 2

Typeset by KEATS, Harrow on the Hill

Printed by Creative Print & Design, Ebbw Vale, Wales for the publishers,

B. T. Batsford, 9 Blenheim Court, Brewery Road,
London N7 9NT

A member of the Chrysalis Group plc

Editor: Phil King

FOREWORD

Michelle has played Acol throughout her distinguished bridge career. Not only does this make her unique amongst top British players, but it also gives her the perfect qualification to write this book.

The methods she teaches are classical, but with a modern touch. Michelle gets right down to the nitty-gritty of basic Acol, highlighting important issues so often overlooked in other texts.

Tony Forrester

CONTENTS

PREFACE

There is absolutely no doubt that bridge is a complex game. Why else does it continue to hold everyone's fascination and keep even the experts begging for more?

To become a competent bridge player takes time and effort. If, however, you do not understand the fundamental principles of the game it will be an eternal struggle.

This book is aimed at the improver. You have already been taught the mechanics of the game and many of the basic requirements to have the pleasure of calling yourself a bridge player.

You probably know what to do with certain types of hands but do you know why it is right? You may be able to reasonably describe the hand you hold to partner, but can you picture the hand partner is describing to you?

While there are numerous bids at your disposal to aid your task, you can never be precise. Your aim, therefore, is to select the best bid available when it is your turn to call in the hope that the message you send will be the most informative.

It's time to throw away your beginner's mantle. Understanding the foundation of the Acol system will be the single most important part of your development. Basic principles need to be ingrained in your memory forever.

Bridge is supposed to be a game. It is difficult, though, to enjoy playing games if you don't understand the rules. While, indeed, it is labelled as complex, I hope to be able make it appear, well ... not quite so complicated.

I have no illusions about being able to re-invent the wheel. My aim is to put you on the right road with a clear view of your destination. All you have to do is study the Highway Code.

Inevitably there will be hands which are deemed unbiddable. There will always be choices. If the answers to all bridge problems were cut and dried it would be a very boring game.

Luck will frequently play a major part in determining whether you win or lose, but you can assist the lady by using judgement – an acquired skill but, none the less, nothing that can't be cultivated. I hope this book will go some way to help you achieve this goal.

This is not just a reading book. It is also intended to be a reference guide for the serious improver and it could even be used as a teaching manual. The chapters are well-defined and stuffed with detailed explanations and examples. Many of the topics are prefaced with an easy-to-view table. A revision quiz at the end of the book is designed to help you understand what you have read. The book is littered with handy hints, rules and hot tips! What more could you want?

Of course, there are probably 101 books on the market already that are aimed at the improver. So, what will make this one special? Cliché or not, as a successful player I wanted to put something back into the game. More importantly, as a bridge teacher I have yet to find a bridge book that incorporates all my own ideas and pet theories that are, despite being 'personalised', part and parcel of the Acol system.

It works for me. I hope it works for you too. Here it is at last!

INTRODUCTION

Just before you start reading, some points to ponder ...

Having some knowledge of the game will certainly be a comfort to you as you glide through this book. Whether you have actually completed a course of lessons, whether you simply have a vague notion of what it's all about and are curious enough to teach yourself, or whether you have been playing for donkey's years and know you need help – this book will be of great benefit to you.

... but I can only do so much!

- ♣ Variables in the bidding and play manifest themselves in the shape of your partner, your opponents and even your own state of health.
- ♢ Your powers of interpretation in the bidding and play will require different skills – for every hand you ever hold.
- ♡ Some hands will play well in No Trumps while others will have more benefits by preferring a trump suit.
- ♠ Some hands will require oodles of points to help you make your contract while on others you will be able to produce tricks out of thin air.
- ♣ Some days all your decisions will be faultless while on others every choice you make will be catastrophic.
- ♢ Your fate is frequently sealed by your own instincts, gut feelings, ruthless opponents or just the shape of the moon!
- ♡ Consistency is commendable, but flexibility is a virtue.
- ♠ Judgement and skill are frequently punished while carelessness and ignorance go rewarded.
- ♣ But, at the end of the day, human error accounts for most of our mistakes. If only we could avoid the stupidities. Keep on reading and who knows ...

P.S.
Acknowledgements must go to all my pupils who have inspired me to put pen to paper. Special thanks to Joan, Jenny, Thelma and Eve without whose unstinting encouragement I would probably have deprived the world of this masterpiece.

Not least of all I would like to thank John and Kevin who have uncomplainingly covered all my absent teaching sessions while I have spent many months toiling away for you!

You turn the page and WOW – complicated tables. Please don't panic! It's true to say you cannot be a bridge player without understanding the principles of scoring. But, don't worry. These tables are here as a reference guide only! Phew! Panic over.

TRICK SCORE TABLE

... only to be used if your contract makes!

6 tricks plus →	1 = 7	2 = 8	3 = 9	4 = 10	5 = 11	6 = 12	7 = 13
♣	20	40	60	80	100	120	140
♢	20	40	60	80	100	120	140
♡	30	60	90	120	150	180	210
♠	30	60	90	120	150	180	210
NT	40	70	100	130	160	190	220

Partscore
A contract bid at a level which scores less than 100 points

Game
A contract bid at a level which scores at least 100 points

Small Slam
Any contract bid and made at the six level

Grand Slam
Any contract bid and made at the seven level

DUPLICATE BONUS SCORE

Add to trick score

PARTSCORE BONUS

Non-game contracts bid and made

Trick score plus 50

GAME BONUS

Contract bid and made – trick score of 100 or more

Trick score plus 300 if nonvulnerable
Trick score plus 500 if vulnerable

SMALL SLAM BONUS

Contract bid and made at the six level

Trick score plus Game Bonus plus 500 if nonvulnerable
Trick score plus Game Bonus plus 750 if vulnerable

GRAND SLAM BONUS

Contract bid and made at the seven level

Trick score plus Game Bonus plus 1000 if nonvulnerable
Trick score plus Game Bonus plus 1500 if vulnerable

PENALTY SCORES

for not making your contract

	Nonvulnerable			Vulnerable		
	UnX	X	XX	UnX	X	XX
1 down	-50	-100	-200	-100	-200	-400
2 down	-100	-300	-600	-200	-500	-1000
3 down	-150	-500	-1000	-300	-800	-1600
4 down	-200	-800	-1600	-400	-1100	-2200
5 down	-250	-1100	-2200	-500	-1400	-2800
6 down	-300	-1400	-2800	-600	-1700	-3400
7 down	-350	-1700	-3400	-700	-2000	-4000

PREMIUM SCORES

for making doubled overtricks

	Nonvulnerable		Vulnerable	
	X	XX	X	XX
Per overtrick	+100	+200	+200	+400

PLUS EXTRA

50 for making a doubled contract
100 for making a redoubled contract

X = Doubled   XX = Redoubled

Chapter One

OPENING THE BIDDING AT THE ONE LEVEL

SUMMARY TABLE FOR THE OPENER		
Hand Shapes	**HCP ***	**Opening Bid**
Balanced Hands	12-14	INT
4-3-3-3	15-19	4 card suit
4-4-3-2		Highest ranked except ♡ + ♠
5-3-3-2		5 card suit
Semi-balanced Hands	12-19 (11)	
5-4-2-2		Longest suit
6-3-2-2		Longest suit
7-2-2-2		Longest suit
Unbalanced Hands	12-19 (10)(11)	
5-4-3-1		Longest suit
5-5-2-1		Highest ranked except ♣ + ♠
4-4-4-1		4-4-4-1 open ♡ 4-4-1-4 open ♣ 4-1-4-4 open ♣ 1-4-4-4 open ♡
All other shapes containing a singleton or void		Longest suit

* High Card Points

Ace = 4   King = 3   Queen = 2   Jack = 1

The first chapter is all about the requirements for selecting an opening bid at the one level.

(A) BALANCED HANDS

If you hold a hand which does not contain a SINGLETON, a VOID or more than one DOUBLETON it is described as BALANCED. Your hand pattern, perforce, will be either 4-3-3-3, 4-4-3-2 or 5-3-3-2. To open the bidding with a balanced hand you require a minimum of 12 HCP.

Whenever your balanced hand contains either 12, 13 or 14 HCP you MUST open the bidding with 1NT, presenting partner with an accurate picture of your shape and strength. If you forget to make this bid you will be in BIG trouble on the next round of the auction! The benefits of limiting your hand so early in the bidding will become apparent as you progress through the book. (The topic of the Weak No Trump (12-14 HCP) is covered in great depth in Chapter Two.)

Balanced hands which are too strong to be opened 1NT, because they house 15-19 HCP, must be described by first mentioning a suit. Depending on the nature of partner's response, and/or possible interference from the opponents, your rebid will be indicative of your extra strength. More about rebids later.

WITH WHICH SUIT SHOULD YOU OPEN THE BIDDING?

(a)   4-3-3-3 distributions;

Holding the flattest variety of balanced hands you are not blessed with a choice of opening bid. Unfortunately, this will occasionally require you to open the bidding with a poor-quality 4-card suit. C'est la vie.

EXAMPLE HANDS: Select your opening bid.

♠ A32	♠ 9876	♠ 543	♠ KQJ	♠ AJ3
♡ QJ43	♡ Q32	♡ 765	♡ AQJ6	♡ J43
◇ J98	◇ KJ8	◇ AKJ	◇ 876	◇ QJ73
♣ A82	♣ KQJ	♣ KQ54	♣ 432	♣ AJ2
12 HCP	12 HCP	13 HCP	13 HCP	14 HCP

Open 1NT with all of these hands

EXAMPLE HANDS: Select your opening bid.

♠ 974	♠ K32	♠ A53	♠ KQJ	♠ A432
♡ Q72	♡ 9752	♡ A96	♡ AK5	♡ J62
◊ AKJ2	◊ AJ8	◊ KQJ2	◊ A86	◊ AJ2
♣ AJ3	♣ AKJ	♣ K32	♣ J974	♣ AKQ
15 HCP	16 HCP	17 HCP	18 HCP	19 HCP
Open 1◊	Open 1♡	Open 1◊	Open 1♣	Open 1♠

(b) 4-4-3-2 distributions;

Also No Trump-orientated, 4-4-3-2 hands within the 12-14 HCP zone are opened 1NT. Once again stronger hands prepare for a rebid in No Trumps after first opening the bidding with one of a suit. Of course, should an 8-card MAJOR-suit fit be discovered *en route* you may have to change your plans. However, it is worth noting at this point that bidding two suits should, otherwise, be reserved for describing semi-balanced or unbalanced hands.

Faced with a choice of two suits, with which of them should you open the bidding?

> **RULE**
>
> For simplicity and effectiveness open the highest ranked with two 4-card suits EXCEPT when holding hearts and spades.

Priority should be given to locating an 8-card major-suit fit. WHY? Imagine a suit of AKQJ opposite 10987. A combination that will make four tricks in a No Trump contract, but potentially up to eight on a cross-ruff if this suit became trumps! Clearly a bargain in return for requiring an extra trick to achieve the game bonus in a major suit. Therefore, it is preferable to choose the major holding a major-minor combination.

Hands containing both majors should be opened 1♡. This gives partner a chance to either support your hearts when they also hold four of them or respond with 1♠ when they have four or more spades.

With both minors it is unlikely to matter which suit you open. This is because most balanced hands with GAME values and a MINOR suit fit will usually be played in a No Trump contract. While the rule advocates opening 1◊, allow suit-quality to overrule when appropriate.

EXAMPLE HANDS: Select your opening bid.

♠ 53	♠ 864	♠ AQ76	♠ KJ43	♠ A876
♡ 9752	♡ J876	♡ KJ85	♡ AQ	♡ 64
◇ AKJ8	◇ AJ	◇ Q2	◇ J765	◇ K86
♣ A43	♣ KQJ8	♣ J74	♣ Q76	♣ AQJ2
12 HCP	12 HCP	13 HCP	13 HCP	14 HCP

Open 1NT with all of these hands

EXAMPLE HANDS: Select your opening bid.

♠ KQ6	♠ A7	♠ Q72	♠ KJ43	♠ AQ76
♡ KQ	♡ QJ87	♡ AKJ6	♡ 52	♡ A2
◇ QJ52	◇ AQ72	◇ K2	◇ KQ42	◇ QJ4
♣ Q972	♣ K76	♣ A862	♣ AKQ	♣ KQJ2
15 HCP	16 HCP	17 HCP	18 HCP	19 HCP
Open 1◇	Open 1♡	Open 1♡	Open 1♠	Open 1♠

(c)   5-3-3-2 distributions;

Contrary to popular belief 5-3-3-2 shapes are also classically balanced as they conform to the definition. Modern theory correctly suggests an opening bid of 1NT with 12-14 HCP despite holding a 5-card suit – be it a minor or a major. A strong proviso, however, is to modify this decision when your hand contains a good quality 5-card major. Thus, 5-card major suits containing two of the top three honour cards would generally be deemed unsuitable for a 1NT opening bid.

Those of you who have, to date, been taught to start with their 5-card suit holding 12-14 HCP – whatever the quality – should spare a thought for their rebid. The advantage of opening 1NT – quite apart from its PRE-EMPTIVE effect – is to announce a limited hand that is also suitable for play in any one of the four suits; much more descriptive than showing partner an essentially non-balanced hand with a ropey suit!

Talking of rebids you will, likely as not, have to rebid your 5-card suit if you opened this suit and your hand is in the 12-14 HCP range. However, it is quite appropriate for stronger hands to make a rebid in No Trumps.

EXAMPLE HANDS: Select your opening bid.

♠ Q5	♠ 863	♠ J98	♠ Q7654	♠ KJ
♡ J82	♡ J8765	♡ A2	♡ K82	♡ KJ7
◊ J86	◊ AQ2	◊ KQJ93	◊ A2	◊ QJ6
♣ AKJ62	♣ KQ	♣ Q32	♣ A84	♣ QJ876
12 HCP	12 HCP	13 HCP	13 HCP	14 HCP

Open 1NT with all of these hands

EXAMPLE HANDS: Select your opening bid.

♠ 863	♠ AQ954	♠ KQ987	♠ 963	♠ 543
♡ AKJ65	♡ J6	♡ A32	♡ AK532	♡ AQJ54
◊ J72	◊ 765	◊ K53	◊ K7	◊ QJ6
♣ K4	♣ KQ3	♣ J7	♣ QJ6	♣ A3
12 HCP	12 HCP	13 HCP	13 HCP	14 HCP

♠ Q7654	♠ Q5	♠ 98765	♠ AQJ	♠ AKQ
♡ K85	♡ A82	♡ A9	♡ KJ7	♡ J6432
◊ A2	◊ Q86	◊ KQJ	◊ KQ765	◊ A2
♣ AQ4	♣ AKJ62	♣ AQJ	♣ Q3	♣ KQ3
15 HCP	16 HCP	17 HCP	18 HCP	19 HCP

But open the bidding with your 5-card suit on all of these hands.

(B) SEMI-BALANCED HANDS

A hand which is classified as SEMI-BALANCED contains no singleton or void yet has two or three doubletons. Your distribution, therefore, will be either 5-4-2-2, 6-3-2-2 or 7-2-2-2.

Your longest suit will be your automatic choice of opening bid. Holding a one-suited hand of six or more cards you will have an easy rebid. The level of your rebid will depend purely on the strength of your hand. A two-suited hand will aim to show both of its suits providing it is able to express the strength of its hand appropriately. These principles will be fully explained in a later chapter.

While an opening bid at the one level primarily promises between 12 and 19 HCP it is possible to extend these guidelines with hands which are not balanced but clearly have extra playing strength. Until a fit has been located it is always difficult to evaluate the power of a hand. Meanwhile, it is acceptable to add 'distributional' points to your high-card points for the purposes of opening the bidding, providing the majority of your high cards are situated in your long suits. Thus, some hands will be deemed to hold the requirements for a one-level opener with as few as 10 or 11 HCP.

HOT TIP

DISTRIBUTIONAL POINTS – AS OPENER

As a guide to opening the bidding DISTRIBUTIONAL POINTS may be added when long suits are of good quality. (Rule of 20)

If the total number of cards in your two longest suits = 9 (semi-balanced or unbalanced) you may open with 11 HCP. (Total = 20)

> 5-4 shape   Add ONE point
>
> 6-3 shape   Add ONE point
>
> 7-2 shape   Add ONE point

If the total number of cards in your two longest suits = 10 (unbalanced) you may open with as few as 10 HCP. (Total = 20)

> 5-5 shape   Add TWO points
>
> 6-4 shape   Add TWO points
>
> 6-5 shape   Add TWO points
>
> 7-3 shape   Add TWO points

Judgement should be exercised, however, when your shortages contain high-card values.

EXAMPLE HANDS: Select your opening bid.

♠ KQJ8732	♠ A82	♠ J8765	♠ Q3	♠ 82
♡ K7	♡ QJ7654	♡ Q7	♡ J3	♡ AQJ54
◇ 54	◇ K8	◇ AKQ2	◇ KQJ9876	◇ J4
♣ Q2	♣ J7	♣ 65	♣ A2	♣ KQJ4
11 HCP	11 HCP	12 HCP	13 HCP	14 HCP
Open 1♠	Open 1♡	Open 1♠	Open 1◇	Open 1♡

EXAMPLE HANDS: Select your opening bid.

♠ AJ7	♠ AKQJ	♠ A3	♠ Q5	♠ AK9543
♡ K2	♡ 76	♡ K975432	♡ AK	♡ Q86
◇ AJ8642	◇ KQ	◇ AQ	◇ QJ	◇ AK
♣ Q7	♣ J8762	♣ KJ	♣ AQ87654	♣ QJ
15 HCP	16 HCP	17 HCP	18 HCP	19 HCP
Open 1◇	Open 1♣	Open 1♡	Open 1♣	Open 1♠

(C) UNBALANCED HANDS

UNBALANCED hands will always contain a singleton or void. The more common distributions are 5-4-3-1, 6-4-2-1, 6-3-3-1, 5-5-2-1 and 4-4-4-1. A No Trump contract can prove hazardous without sufficient strength between you in all four suits. Your priority here will be to first look for a trump fit before attempting a contract without a trump suit.

Once again, hands containing suits of equal length require a special mention. 5-5 distributions will be best described if both suits can be bid economically.

> ### RULE
>
> Open the highest ranked with two 5-card suits EXCEPT when holding clubs and spades.

The reason for this becomes clearer when you are able to appreciate the requirements for a reverse bid, which will be explained later.

4-4-4-1 shapes are notoriously difficult to handle! Neither balanced nor unbalanced (there is no accurately descriptive rebid) they are undoubtedly the bane of any bridge player's life. Whilst you are unable to open 1NT it is often preferable to rebid No Trumps holding the 15-19 HCP range when partner has bid your singleton. Rebidding a second suit is the only alternative when partner has been unable to either support your suit or bid another that you hold. The reason this choice becomes undesirable, however, is due to the fact that it will distort the picture of your hand. Partner is entitled to expect nine cards in the two suits you bid and may be disappointed to see otherwise. So be it. It's something that even the experts have to live with so you'll just have to do the best you can.

Controversy surrounds the choice of suit to open with this shape. Providing you have a sensible rebid when partner bids your singleton it is difficult to lay down the law, except to say it is never correct to open 1♠.

RULE

Let's make it easy. With a black singleton open 1♡ and with a red singleton open 1♣.

EXAMPLE HANDS: Select your opening bid.

♠ J876	♠ KJ85	♠ KQ73	♠ K	♠ Q765
♡ AKJ2	♡ KJ64	♡ J	♡ K752	♡ J876
◇ K765	◇ 7	◇ AQ87	◇ AKJ4	◇ A
♣ 9	♣ AJ54	♣ Q654	♣ J852	♣ AKQ7
12 HCP	13 HCP	14 HCP	15 HCP	16 HCP
Open 1♡	Open 1♣	Open 1♣	Open 1♡	Open 1♣

EXAMPLE HANDS: Select your opening bid.

♠ 652	♠ 6	♠ AKJ65	♠ K4	♠ KQJ63
♡ AJ987	♡ Q2	♡ KQJ72	♡ A8765	♡ Q2
◇ -	◇ K8765	◇ 432	◇ AKQ32	◇ A
♣ AQ863	♣ AQJ87	♣ -	♣ 4	♣ KQJ76
11 HCP	12 HCP	14 HCP	16 HCP	18 HCP
Open 1♡	Open 1◇	Open 1♠	Open 1♡	Open 1♣

EXAMPLE HANDS: Select your opening bid.

♠ AQ765	♠ Q654	♠ 6	♠ -	♠ J97654
♡ KJ86	♡ -	♡ A97654	♡ AQ	♡ KJ
◇ Q43	◇ AKQJ	◇ KQ7	◇ QJ8765	◇ A
♣ 7	♣ J8765	♣ AJ6	♣ AQ987	♣ AKJ5
12 HCP	13 HCP	14 HCP	15 HCP	17 HCP
Open 1♠	Open 1♣	Open 1♡	Open 1◇	Open 1♠

EXAMPLE HANDS: Select your opening bid.

♠ 5	♠ AQJ54	♠ Q	♠ KQ5	♠ 9
♡ KQ8765	♡ 73	♡ J8765	♡ K86	♡ AQJ7
◇ 86	◇ K9876	◇ KJ	◇ QJ9843	◇ A9864
♣ AJ74	♣ 8	♣ QJ742	♣ 3	♣ 876
10 HCP	10 HCP	10 HCP	11 HCP	11 HCP
Open 1♡	Open 1♠	Pass	Open 1◇	Open 1◇

Notice how the stronger distributional hands exude so much more playing strength than the balanced variety. If these hands can find a trump fit their power extends even further beyond the normal boundaries. Therefore, with shapely hands concealing substantial trick-taking potential, you must consider opening the bidding at the two level. See Chapter Seven.

RULE

After an opening bid of a suit at the one level you will be expected to make another bid UNLESS:

(a) Partner passes.
(b) Partner has made a limit response.
(c) The opponents have intervened.

Your rebid options will be explained soon.

HANDY HINTS

Open the highest of two 4-card suits except ♡ + ♠

Open the highest of two 5-card suits except ♣ + ♠

The distribution for a 1NT opener can include a 5-card suit.

A combined total of 25 points is required to attempt game. This may be a combination of high-card points and distributional points.

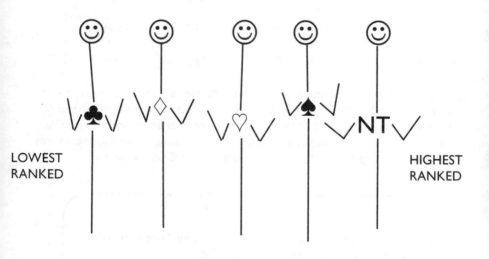

LOWEST RANKED   HIGHEST RANKED

Colonel Club   Colonel Diamond   Colonel Heart   Colonel Spade   Colonel No Trump

Chapter Two

OPENING BALANCED HANDS WITH 12-14 HCP

SUMMARY TABLE FOR RESPONDING TO A 1NT OPENER
With less than 12 HCP and a balanced hand you must PASS at your turn to open the bidding.
12 - 14 HCP and a balanced hand – OPEN 1NT

RESPONDING TO A 1NT OPENER

0 - 10 HCP

Pass	Without 5+ cards in ◇, ♡ or ♠
2◇, 2♡, 2♠	With a 5+ card suit
2♣	Stayman convention

11 - 12 HCP

2NT	Balanced
2♣	Stayman convention

13+ HCP

3NT	Balanced (13-18 HCP)
3♣ 3◇	6+ card suit, unbalanced
3♡ 3♠	5 card suit
4♡ 4♠	6+ card suit
2♣	Stayman convention

A combined total of 25 points is required to attempt game

(A) THE 1NT OPENING BID AND RESPONSES

If you have remembered nothing else from your first few bridge lessons, the opening bid of 1NT has surely survived your memory test! It is the highest bid you can open at the one level.

The structure of the ACOL system revolves around the meaning of this bid.

First a reminder of its definition:

> ### RULE
>
> An opening bid of 1NT shows 12-14 HCP and a BALANCED hand. It is a LIMIT bid. A LIMIT bid is defined as describing the strength of a hand within a narrow band of points. A limit bid may be weak or strong, but it is NON-FORCING.

It is not necessary for the 1NT opener to have an HONOUR CARD in every suit. Hands where you will be required to hold a "STOP" (i.e. an Ace, King, Queen or Jack) in a particular suit will be given a special mention when applicable. Suffice to say that while a stop may temporarily prevent a defensive onslaught in an otherwise weak suit it may not be able to assist you in your effort to develop tricks.

Having already described your hand so accurately with a bid of 1NT it is clearly sensible for your partner – who is so far UNLIMITED – to control the rest of the auction for your side. The partner of the limit bidder can aptly be called 'the captain of the ship' as, armed with the knowledge of his/her side's combined strength, s/he is in the best position to steer the auction for you.

Weak or strong the captain also has significantly more information than the opposition! While the subsequent auction will help to reveal clues about much of your side's assets the opponents are often left to drown in a sea of uncertainty.

TIME TO PUT YOURSELF IN THE CAPTAIN'S SHOES ...

(1) HANDS IN THE 0-10 HCP ZONE

Remembering that you need 25 points to attempt game there is little chance of achieving the number of tricks thus required when you have between 0 and 10 HCP. The best course of action, therefore, is to settle for the best available PARTSCORE. Holding a modest collection of points does not preclude you from bidding. Of course, it may not always be possible to produce a plus score for your side and your minus score should, therefore, not necessarily be considered disastrous.

(a) PASS

Holding a balanced hand without a 5-card or longer suit you must be content to play the hand in a No Trump contract despite relative weakness. It is unlikely that you will be bidding again in the subsequent auction should the opponents compete.

(b) 2◊ 2♡ 2♠

Nominating your 5+ card suit at the two level signals weakness and requests the 1NT opener to PASS. Known as a weak takeout this bid is a SIGN-OFF. Partner is not permitted to bid again even though s/he may only have two small trumps. With a particularly weak hand it will be difficult to produce anything like seven tricks in 1NT. Played in a suit contract, however, there is more scope for making tricks by way of trumping your losers. This factor alone compensates for being a level higher. Depending on the strength of your hand you may wish to compete later in the auction, but your partner – who opened 1NT – is NOT invited to the party! (You will be shown how to bid hands with 0-10 HCP and 5+ clubs in the chapter on Stayman.)

(c) 2♣

The Stayman convention requests information about 4-card majors. It can also be used to show a weak hand with clubs. (The second part of this chapter is dedicated to Stayman.)

EXAMPLE HANDS: Partner opens 1NT. What is your response?

♠ 543	♠ 86	♠ 965	♠ AJ987	♠ Q976
♡ 865	♡ 43	♡ J87652	♡ 7	♡ A54
◊ 9862	◊ 98765	◊ Q53	◊ K865	◊ K84
♣ 532	♣ 5432	♣ 6	♣ 876	♣ J54
0 HCP	0 HCP	3 HCP	8 HCP	10 HCP
Pass	Bid 2◊	Bid 2♡	Bid 2♠	Pass

> ## RULE
>
> Partner is commanded to PASS your 'Weak Takeout' bid at the two level in ◊, ♡ or ♠.

(2) HANDS IN THE 11-12 HCP ZONE

In order to ascertain whether the partnership holds the requisite combined 25 points to attempt game you need to send partner an invitation.

(a) 2NT

This bid shows either 11 or 12 HCP and a balanced hand that has no interest in locating a trump fit. In response, the 1NT opener must PASS holding a minimum, i.e. 12 HCP and accept the invitation to game by bidding 3NT with a maximum ie. 14 HCP. What about hands with 13 HCP? Evaluation of hands in this category require extra detail. If you can't wait, turn to the third part of this chapter!

(b) 2♣

The Stayman convention requesting information about 4-card majors. (All will be revealed soon.)

EXAMPLE HANDS: Partner opens 1NT. What is your response?

♠ A654	♠ J7	♠ 987	♠ A53	♠ KQ9
♡ K87	♡ AQJ	♡ QJ7	♡ Q54	♡ 87
◊ Q87	◊ J7543	◊ K72	◊ Q2	◊ AK82
♣ Q32	♣ Q98	♣ AQ52	♣ KJ762	♣ 7654
11 HCP	11 HCP	12 HCP	12 HCP	12 HCP
2NT	2NT	2NT	2NT	2NT

Partner is expected to PASS with a minimum and bid 3NT with a maximum.

(3) HANDS IN THE 13+ HCP ZONE

Holding 13 or more points tells you that the partnership is in possession of at least 25 HCP. Prospects of game are good. You may already have a clear idea of the best game contract, in which case you can go straight there! With hands that need more information before making a decision there is a range of bids at your disposal to help you explore.

(a)   3NT

Restricted to a point range of 13-18 this game call is a SIGN-OFF which partner is obliged to pass. It generally describes a balanced type of hand, although it will frequently include an unbalanced hand with six clubs or diamonds.

(b)   3♣   3◇

With no upper point limit these calls are NATURAL with at least six cards in the bid suit and are FORCING TO GAME. Minor-suited hands are, more often than not, best played in a No Trump contract. Not only does this achieve a bigger score, but fewer tricks are required for a game bonus. Hence, this bid is not often used unless the hand is either very distributional or SLAM-orientated.

(c)   3♡   3♠

Looking for an 8-card major-suit fit a bid of 3♡ or 3♠ shows precisely five cards in that suit. As the 1NT opener, you are simply requested to raise to game in the bid suit if you hold three or more of them or return to 3NT with only two.

(d)   4♡   4♠

A natural call showing a limited hand with at least six cards in the bid suit. With no desire to explore for a slam this is another example of a sign-off bid which opener is requested to pass. Responder knows that opener has at least two cards in the major and believes that this will be a safer game than 3NT.

(e)   2♣

Guess what! Not long to wait now ...

EXAMPLE HANDS: Partner opens 1NT. What is your response?

♠ A753	♠ AQ	♠ Q3	♠ KQ	♠ AJ3
♡ Q76	♡ K72	♡ A2	♡ AJ	♡ Q94
◇ 987	◇ J8	◇ KQ642	◇ QJ5432	◇ KJ
♣ AK6	♣ KJ8765	♣ KJ76	♣ QJ6	♣ AQ643
13 HCP	14 HCP	15 HCP	16 HCP	17 HCP
3NT	3NT	3NT	3NT	3NT

EXAMPLE HANDS: Partner opens 1NT. What is your response?

♠ 732	♠ -	♠ Q	♠ AJ865	♠ KQ5
♡ KQJ86	♡ J76	♡ AK9764	♡ Q2	♡ 8
◇ A9	◇ AQJ975	◇ Q32	◇ AQ87	◇ A65
♣ K42	♣ KQJ4	♣ K85	♣ Q3	♣ AKJ876
13 HCP	14 HCP	14 HCP	15 HCP	17 HCP
3♡	3◇	4♡	3♠	3♣

HANDY HINTS

Balanced hands require 12 HCP to open the bidding.

Limit bidders do not bid again unless requested by partner.

A SIGN-OFF tells partner not to bid again!

Moderate hands with minor-suit fits should prefer a No Trump contract.

You do not guarantee stops in every suit to open 1NT.

A combined total of 25 points is required to attempt game.

STOP PRESS ...

SLAM BIDDING

It will not have escaped your attention that there has been no mention of hands that are strong enough to attempt a slam. Bidding slams is a specialised topic. Chapter Ten is dedicated to the task of explaining this theme.

(B) THE STAYMAN CONVENTION

When partner opens 1NT (whatever the strength) you need to know how to locate a 4-4 major suit fit when your hand has a SHORTAGE and, therefore, a No Trump contract may be unsafe. You cannot introduce a bid of hearts or spades without promising at least a 5-card suit, so what is the solution?

The STAYMAN convention, (named after the American bridge player Samuel Stayman), was designed to come to the rescue. In response to a 1NT opening, a bid of 2♣ is ARTIFICIAL, says nothing about clubs, and asks partner if s/he has a 4-card major.

OPENER'S RESPONSE TO THE 2♣ ENQUIRY:

2♦ = No 4-card major.

2♡ = Shows 4 hearts. May have 4 spades.

2♠ = Shows 4 spades. Denies 4 hearts.

The 2♣ bidder does not promise any points. However, s/he must be able to cope with any response by opener and, therefore, the hand will contain either:

(a) One or two 4-card majors and 11+ HCP.

♠ A876	♠ KQJ4	♠ 4	♠ KJ76	♠ Q765
♡ QJ86	♡ 54	♡ AK54	♡ 43	♡ J865
◇ K5	◇ A765	◇ Q8765	◇ AQJ7	◇ AKQ
♣ J54	♣ Q76	♣ A87	♣ K87	♣ K2
11 HCP	12 HCP	13 HCP	14 HCP	15 HCP

(b) One 5-card major and 11-12 HCP.

♠ Q8732	♠ 2	♠ AJ654	♠ KQJ	♠ KJ765
♡ Q98	♡ AKJ73	♡ J8	♡ J8742	♡ 9
◇ A5	◇ Q32	◇ KJ5	◇ A43	◇ AK83
♣ K54	♣ J864	♣ J42	♣ J7	♣ J43
11 HCP	11 HCP	11 HCP	12 HCP	12 HCP

(c)   Zero+ points but at least 5-4 in BOTH majors or;
      4-4 in BOTH majors plus a 5-card diamond suit.

♠ 98765	♠ J876	♠ QJ86	♠ AKQ3	♠ AKJ7
♡ 5432	♡ J876	♡ AJ876	♡ KQJ87	♡ KQJ76
◇ 32	◇ J7654	◇ J52	◇ 8	◇ 76
♣ 32	♣ -	♣ 3	♣ J86	♣ Q2
0 HCP	3 HCP	9 HCP	16 HCP	16 HCP

(d)   A 6+ card club suit and less than 11 HCP.

♠ 76	♠ 32	♠ 4	♠ K87	♠ QJ
♡ 54	♡ QJ8	♡ AJ54	♡ 4	♡ Q8
◇ Q7	◇ 87	◇ 54	◇ J32	◇ K8
♣ Q876543	♣ K98765	♣ QJ8765	♣ AJ8765	♣ J876543
4 HCP	6 HCP	8 HCP	9 HCP	9 HCP

All these examples conform to the requirements for using Stayman.

RESPONSES BY THE STAYMAN BIDDER and continuations;

After partner has responded to your STAYMAN 2♣ enquiry you need to complete the picture of your hand.

(1) HANDS IN THE 0-10 HCP ZONE
(a)   Pass

Promising 4-card support for partner's major suit after a 2♡ or 2♠ response or a 5-card diamond suit after a 2◇ response.

(b)   2♡ 2♠

Following a 2◇ denial, you are now confirming a weak hand with a minimum of five cards in your bid major and four cards in the other one. It is a SIGN-OFF, requesting partner to pass.

(c)   3♣

The only way to express a weak hand with clubs. "Sorry partner, I have no interest in your major-suit holdings. PLEASE PASS!". As this contract is to be played at the three level it is advisable to have at least six clubs and a handful of points. Weaker hands with clubs should pass 1NT.

EXAMPLE AUCTIONS: As responder to partner's opening bid of 1NT.

♠ Q9843   1NT - 2♣* - 2♡ - Pass
♡ KJ42
◊ 54   A hand on which you would have bid 2♠ over a 2◊
♣ 65   response. Now delighted to play in hearts.

♠ J765   1NT - 2♣* - 2♠ - Pass
♡ J5432
◊ 54   Similarly, you have successfully located a spade
♣ 65   fit rather than gamble a 2♡ contract over 1NT.

♠ K7542   1NT - 2♣* - 2◊*- 2♡/2♠
♡ Q8642
◊ 2   A weak takeout requesting partner to pass.
♣ 32

♠ KQ54   1NT - 2♣* - 2◊*- Pass
♡ Q432
◊ Q8654   Although partner's 2◊ response was conventional
♣ -   you can be guaranteed at least a 7-card fit.

♠ 83   1NT - 2♣* - 2◊*- 3♣
♡ K6
◊ J32   A weak take-out requesting partner to pass.
♣ QJ9876

(2) HANDS IN THE 11-12 HCP ZONE
(a)   2NT
In reply to 2◊ 2♡ or 2♠ this bid covers all hand patterns in the 11-12 HCP
range that have not yet located a major-suit fit. Essentially balanced (it may
have a 5-card major) 2NT denies a fit in partner's bid major and INVITES
game in No Trumps (or spades if opener responded 2♡) opposite a
maximum 1NT. After a 2♡ response the opener is obliged to correct the
contract to spades at the appropriate level if s/he holds four of them too.

(b)   3♡ 3♠

A raise of partner's suit to the three level confirms the 8-card fit and invites game opposite a maximum.

EXAMPLE AUCTIONS: As responder to partner's opening bid of 1NT.

♠ AJ76   1NT - 2♣* - 2◊*- 2NT
♡ KQ42
◊ J87   Opener is requested to pass with a minimum and bid
♣ 32   3NT with a maximum.

♠ J9642   1NT - 2♣* - 2◊*- 2NT
♡ Q65
◊ K7   Opener is requested to pass with a minimum and bid
♣ AJ3   3NT with a maximum.

♠ KJ6   1NT - 2♣* - 2♠ - 2NT
♡ J543
◊ Q543   Opener has denied four cards in hearts and is
♣ AJ   requested to pass with a minimum or bid 3NT
            with a maximum.

♠ A975   1NT - 2♣* - 2♡ - 2NT
♡ 73
◊ A32   Opener is requested to pass with a minimum and bid
♣ K765   3NT with a maximum. BUT if opener holds both majors
            s/he must convert to 3♠ with a minimum or 4♠ with a
            maximum.

♠ QJ75   1NT - 2♣* - 2♠ - 3♠
♡ J6
◊ KQ54   Agreeing spades as trumps you are now inviting
♣ Q32   partner to bid 4♠ with a maximum but pass if minimum.

♠ AQ73   1NT - 2♣* - 2♡ - 3♡
♡ K852
◊ Q5   Another example of an invitational raise.
♣ J94

(3) HANDS IN THE 13+ HCP ZONE

(a)   3♡ 3♠

A bid of 3♡ or 3♠ following a 2◊ response promises the values for at least game and 5 cards in the bid suit. Deduction will tell you that this call will also show 4 cards in the other major too, else you would have made an immediate jump response over 1NT. The only information you require now is the number of cards partner holds in your suit. Partner should raise the major to game with 3 and return to 3NT with only 2.

(b) 3NT

A sign-off? Well, sort of. After a 2◊ or 2♠ response – yes. After a 2♡ response it is a sign-off providing your partner does not hold a 4-card spade suit too. With both majors partner is obliged to convert 3NT to 4♠.

(c) 3◊

A natural and game-forcing manoeuvre with at least 5 diamonds and a 4-card major. Once again, a probe for game in a minor suit suggests extreme distribution and/or slam ambitions.

(d) 4♡ 4♠

Bingo! A fit, a game and I'm content to let you play the hand.

EXAMPLE AUCTIONS: As responder to partner's opening bid of 1NT.

♠ KJ75   1NT - 2♣* - 2◊*- 3♡
♡ QJ876
◊ A3   "Partner, I know you do not have a 4-card major, but
♣ K7   please tell me if you have 3-card support for my 5-card
            heart suit. Bid 4♡ if you have and 3NT if you haven't."

♠ AQJ86   1NT - 2♣* - 2◊*- 3♠
♡ KQJ8
◊ 432   Same message as above with a 5-card spade suit.
♣ 8

♠ KQ73   1NT - 2♣* - 2◊*- 3NT
♡ AJ52
◊ J   A clear-cut sign-off.
♣ QJ43

♠ KQ73   INT - 2♣* - 2♡ - 3NT
♡ J85
◇ A5   3NT is a sign-off as long as partner is not lurking with
♣ QJ42   a 4-card spade suit!

♠ 65   INT - 2♣* - 2♡ - 4♡
♡ AQJ8
◇ KQ94   Content to play a game in hearts. A sign-off.
♣ K92

♠ AK95   INT - 2♣* - 2♠ - 4♠
♡ 98532
◇ 7   A routine raise to game in spades.
♣ AQ2

♠ A   INT - 2♣* - 2♠ - 3◇
♡ KQ32
◇ AKJ765   Promising hearts and diamonds you are now expressing
♣ 32   interest in a diamond game or possibly a slam.

HOT TIP

If partner has not shown four cards in your 4-card major do not bid them yourself. Unless you rebid 3♣ – which is specifically to play and shows no major suit interest – you have already shown that you hold a 4-card major by virtue of having used Stayman!

HANDY HINTS

No shortage (fewer than 3 cards), no Stayman.

Stayman 2♣ does not apply after intervention.

Stayman does not replace your other options over 1NT. It is merely an enhancement.

Do not use the 2♣ convention when you cannot sensibly control the subsequent auction.

You can use Stayman with NO POINTS!

SUMMARY OF REBIDS FOR THE STAYMAN BIDDER		
IF YOU HAVE LOCATED A MAJOR SUIT FIT		
a) 0-10 HCP	Pass	*(To play)*
b) 11-12 HCP	Raise major to 3 level	*(Invitational)*
c) 13+ HCP	Raise major to 4 level	*(Game)*
IF YOU HAVE NOT LOCATED A MAJOR SUIT FIT		
a) 0-10 HCP	Rebid two of your 5-card suit	*(To play)*
b) 0-10 HCP	Rebid 3♣ with 6+ clubs	*(To play)*
c) 11-12 HCP	Rebid 2NT	*(Invitational)*
d) 13+ HCP	Rebid 3NT (no 5-card major)	*(Game)*
	Rebid three of your 5-card major if 5-4 in both majors	*(Forcing to game)*
	Rebid 3◊ with diamonds and a major	*(Forcing to game)*

Other schools of thought may advocate variations of the Stayman convention, all equally acceptable.

e.g.   1NT-2♣-2◊-3♡/♠ can be played as invitational with a 5-card major.

1NT-2♣-2◊-3◊ can then be used as an extension to Stayman requesting opener to bid a 3-card major for when responder is 5-4 or 5-5 in the majors with game going values ...

... and there's more – all food for thought! Whichever method you do decide to adopt, it helps to discuss your choice first with partner, who may have ideas of their own!

[More advanced players will be keen to incorporate the Transfer System into their repertoire. While transfers offer significant advantages, they are an unnecessary burden on your memory at this stage of your development.]

(C) HAND EVALUATION

... or how to appreciate the beauty of your bridge hand!

Great emphasis is placed on reaching 25-point games. While a 12-14 1NT opening bid limits your hand to a 3-point range it is still difficult to guarantee the magic formula unless you actually hold 13 HCP as responder.

Inviting with 11-12 HCP leaves partner with the unenviable task of guessing whether it is actually 11 or 12 when they have opened with 13. Does it really matter?

Your limited experience has undoubtedly warned you already that some games can be made with fewer than 25 points while others flounder with a great deal more. Such are the vagaries of bridge.

But, like 'art appreciation' there is far more depth to a hand than just looking at the picture.

Devoting a section to valuing balanced hands with 13 HCP in particular may seem a trifle eccentric. On the contrary. You can use your acquired skill for hand evaluation in other situations too, so whatever you learn here will serve you in good stead.

(1) INTERMEDIATE CARDS

Compare the following pairs of hands in a 3NT contract:

(a)

♠ K53	♠ AQ2
♡ Q654	♡ J32
◇ AQ	◇ KJ54
♣ Q943	♣ J76

Opener – 13 HCP   Responder – 12 HCP

1NT - 2NT - ?

(b)

♠ K53	♠ AQ2
♡ Q1098	♡ J32
◇ AQ	◇ KJ54
♣ Q943	♣ J76

Opener – 13 HCP   Responder – 12 HCP

1NT - 2NT - ?

Quite a difference considering that superficially they are identical! The first example has seven obvious winners and guess work, luck, or a possible defensive mistake might allow your game contract to prevail.

Example (b), by comparison, is poetry in motion. Nine tricks look a pretty good prospect. What's the difference? The spot cards in hearts – i.e. the presence of the 10 and the 9 solidify an otherwise anaemic suit and make it possible to produce two tricks safely.

HOT TIP

The presence of tens and nines clearly improves the playing strength of a hand. Accept the invitation holding intermediate cards.

Here are a selection of 1NT openers with 13 HCP on which you should accept the invitation to game after a 2NT enquiry.

♠ AJ108	♠ K53	♠ Q987	♠ 86	♠ KJ102
♡ J1097	♡ J6	♡ AJ98	♡ A108	♡ K95
◇ QJ5	◇ KQ98	◇ K2	◇ Q9876	◇ J107
♣ A4	♣ A987	♣ K87	♣ AK6	♣ KQ7

(2) LONG SUITS

4-3-3-3 hands are of little use when attempting to develop tricks while a 1NT opener with a 5-card suit is instantly promotable. In much the same way 4-4-3-2 shapes are also of greater value as you have the potential to develop two suits.

HOT TIP

A source of tricks will be significant in determining your success in 3NT.

These hands are worth a raise to 3NT after partner has invited game:

♠ K9754	♠ 953	♠ KQ2	♠ KJ76	♠ Q75
♡ K2	♡ A6	♡ Q63	♡ AK54	♡ AJ532
◇ Q98	◇ QJ83	◇ KQJ43	◇ 75	◇ KJ7
♣ AJ4	♣ AQ76	♣ 65	♣ Q98	♣ Q8

(3) POSITION OF HONOUR CARDS

Compare these two sets of hands in a 3NT contract:

(c)

♠ 8432   ♠ QJ
♡ 8765   ♡ K94
◇ AQ   ◇ K1097
♣ AK3   ♣ QJ54

Opener – 13 HCP   Responder – 12 HCP

1NT - 2NT - ?

(d)

♠ AK65   ♠ QJ
♡ AQ65   ♡ K94
◇ 84   ◇ K1097
♣ 876   ♣ QJ54

Opener – 13 HCP   Responder – 12 HCP

1NT - 2NT - ?

Game is clearly more attractive with example (d) and would merit a raise to 3NT. Why? Because scope for developing tricks was enhanced when the high cards in the short suits were transferred to the long suits.

> ## HOT TIP
>
> Honour cards are more precious situated in long suits than short suits. The stronger your long suit is, the more power you have in its establishment.

A variation on this theme finds that certain combinations of honour cards have more productive qualities than others:

(e)

♠ KJ2   ♠ A53
♡ KJ76   ♡ 953
◇ KJ2   ◇ A85
♣ J43   ♣ A762

Opener – 13 HCP   Responder – 12 HCP

1NT - 2NT - ?

(f)
♠ 762	♠ A53
♡ K7	♡ 953
◇ KQ42	◇ A85
♣ KQ43	♣ A762

Opener – 13 HCP   Responder – 12 HCP

INT - 2NT - ?

On a bad day you will struggle to make INT with example (e) whereas example (f) offers excellent chances for a game bonus.

The difference lies in the compatability of the honour cards. K-J holdings are weak without the Queen opposite. Similarly A-J or A-Q combinations can be relatively useless without the aid of the King.

HOT TIP

Honour cards are much more useful when they are not split.

HOT TIP

When do you need to evaluate?

You should use judgement to help you decide whether ...

a)   ... to open the bidding or to Pass.
b)   ... you are minimum or maximum.
c)   ... you should overcall or Pass.
d)   ... you should play or defend after competition.

Clearly, two balanced hands sit precariously on the fence of success with only 25 HCP to their credit. So, remember these words of wisdom;

HANDY HINTS

A good hand contains intermediate cards.
A good hand contains long suits for development.
A good hand prefers honour cards in its long suits.
A good hand sees its honour cards working together.

Chapter Three

RESPONDING TO A SUIT OPENING BID

```
                              RULE

You MUST reply to a one of a suit opening bid holding 6 or more
HCP ... a logical conclusion when the opener could be
concealing as many as 19 HCP.
```

As well as determining your side's combined point count, your aim is to locate a trump fit – preferably in a major – or look for a No Trump contract. This does not mean you should ignore minor suits. Without game values it is often preferable to subside in a minor suit partscore even though club and diamond contracts do not score as many points.

Having established that you must reply with 6 or more HCP you need to know HOW, but, first of all, a reminder of why partner has opened the bidding with one of a suit.

a) S/he holds a balanced hand with 15-19 HCP that is too strong to be opened 1NT.

or b) S/he holds a semi-balanced or unbalanced hand and 10-19 HCP.

Whatever the reason, partner will have a minimum of 12 HCP (or its distributional equivalent) and usually a maximum of 19 HCP.

WHAT ARE YOUR OPTIONS AS RESPONDER?

1) You should PASS with less than 6 HCP.

2) You can raise partner's suit with 6+ HCP and 4+ support.
This is a LIMIT BID and it is NON-FORCING.

3) You can bid No Trumps with 6+ HCP.
This is a LIMIT BID and it is NON-FORCING.

4) You can change the suit which promises at least 6 HCP.
This bid is UNLIMITED and, therefore, FORCING.

WITH SUPPORT FOR PARTNER

(A) HOLDING 4-CARD SUPPORT FOR PARTNER'S MAJOR

If partner opens 1♡ or 1♠ and you have at least four of them TOO, you should support your partner immediately.

It doesn't matter if you have another suit which is longer.

The level you respond at is determined by your point count.

These bids are limited and non-forcing.

a)	6-9	HCP	=	Raise 1♡/1♠ to 2♡/2♠
b)	10-12	HCP	=	Raise 1♡/1♠ to 3♡/3♠
c)	13-15	HCP	=	Raise 1♡/1♠ to 4♡/4♠ GAME.

Hands with 4-card support for partner's major and 16+ HCP will initially change the suit. This aspect will be covered in much greater depth in Chapter Nine on JUMP SHIFTS.

EXAMPLE HANDS: Partner opens 1♡. What do you respond?

♠ 87	♠ Q6543	♠ 4	♠ Q54	♠ A7
♡ AQ52	♡ K432	♡ AKJ2	♡ QJ742	♡ AJ87
◊ 654	◊ Q3	◊ Q987	◊ KJ7	◊ K5432
♣ 9876	♣ J6	♣ 8543	♣ QJ	♣ Q2
6 HCP	8 HCP	10 HCP	12 HCP	14 HCP
2♡	2♡	3♡	3♡	4♡

EXAMPLE HANDS: Partner opens 1♠. What do you respond?

♠ K642	♠ AQJ3	♠ QJ64	♠ Q9732	♠ AK86
♡ 432	♡ 43	♡ A432	♡ J76	♡ AJ53
◊ 654	◊ J543	◊ 654	◊ KJ	◊ J
♣ 862	♣ 852	♣ Q2	♣ A42	♣ 8765
3 HCP	8 HCP	9 HCP	11 HCP	13 HCP
Pass	2♠	2♠	3♠	4♠

CONTINUATIONS BY OPENER

The ball is back in opener's court. Having discovered that you hold an 8-card major-suit fit your next task is to play at the right level. Partscore? Game? or Slam?

OPTIONS AS OPENER AFTER A RAISE TO THE TWO LEVEL: (6-9 HCP)

1♡ - 2♡ - ?	1♠ - 2♠ - ?

1) 10-15 HCP   -   PASS
With no hope of a 25-point game stay as low as possible.

2) 16-18 HCP   -   INVITE WITH A RAISE TO THREE
                        -           INVITE via 2NT if balanced
                        -           INTRODUCE A NEW SUIT.
With a glimmer of hope opposite a maximum, non-balanced hands should make a game-invitational bid with a raise to the three level, or introduce a new suit as a trial-bid. Partner should accept with 8 or 9 HCP, or with a useful holding in the trial-bid suit. Balanced hands with 17 or 18 HCP should invite with 2NT, but pass with only 16 HCP.

3) 19 HCP   -   BID GAME
With a clear message of at least 25 HCP go straight to game.

OPTIONS AFTER A RAISE TO THE THREE LEVEL: (10-12 HCP)

1♡ - 3♡ - ?	1♠ - 3♠ - ?

1) 13 or fewer HCP   -   PASS
Opposite an average of 11 HCP it is generally best policy to PASS and take a probable plus score.

2) 14+ HCP   -   BID GAME
When partner tables only 10 HCP your declarer play may be tested but otherwise you have two chances of landing in at least a 25-point game. The game bonus makes the small risk worthwhile.

3) 19 HCP   -   CONSIDER SLAM PROSPECTS
Touching the 30-point zone your hand may be suitable for an attempt to make a slam. More about those later ...

HOT TIP

DISTRIBUTIONAL POINTS – AS RESPONDER

With an unbalanced hand and a MAJOR-SUIT fit your hand may be worth an upgrade. (Exclude 4-4-4-1 patterns).

Add ONE point for a small doubleton.

Add TWO points for a singleton.

Add THREE points for a void.

Judgement should be exercised, however, when your shortages contain high-card values.

EXAMPLE HANDS: Make your rebid as opener after 1♡ - 2♡ - ?

♠ 76	♠ QJ8	♠ AQ7	♠ 5	♠ AJ
♡ AK7652	♡ KQJ43	♡ AJ8765	♡ A8753	♡ AJ864
◊ A86	◊ J2	◊ 4	◊ KJ54	◊ KQ3
♣ Q3	♣ A63	♣ KJ6	♣ AKJ	♣ A73

13 HCP	14 HCP	15 HCP	16 HCP	19 HCP

Pass	Pass	3♡	3♡	4♡

EXAMPLE HANDS: Make your rebid as opener after 1♠ - 2♠ - ?

♠ AKJ32	♠ J9876	♠ K8642	♠ Q7642	♠ KQJ87
♡ KJ87	♡ QJ8	♡ 84	♡ A3	♡ KJ2
◊ 65	◊ AKQ6	◊ AK92	◊ KQJ7	◊ AKJ8
♣ 87	♣ 2	♣ AJ	♣ KJ	♣ 2

12 HCP	13 HCP	15 HCP	16 HCP	18 HCP

Pass	Pass	3♠	3♠	4♠

EXAMPLE HANDS: Make your rebid as opener after 1♡ - 3♡ - ?

♠ 76	♠ K	♠ 76	♠ 2	♠ K62
♡ AQ876	♡ J7654	♡ AK7652	♡ J8765	♡ AKQ52
◇ QJ87	◇ KJ43	◇ A86	◇ KQ42	◇ Q65
♣ Q7	♣ KJ2	♣ Q3	♣ AK7	♣ 54
11 HCP	12 HCP	13 HCP	13 HCP	14 HCP
Pass	Pass	4♡	4♡	4♡

(B) HOLDING 4-CARD SUPPORT FOR PARTNER'S MINOR

If partner opens 1♣ or 1◇ and you have four of them too your response should depend on whether you also hold a 4-card major.

Priority should be given to finding a trump fit in hearts or spades as your partner may hold two suits.

Therefore, after an opening bid of 1♣ or 1◇ by partner, you should respond 1♡ or 1♠ holding at least four of that suit in preference to supporting partner's minor.

If your hand is best described by supporting partner's minor suit the responses are as follows:

a)   6-9 points   =   Raise 1♣/1◇ to 2♣/2◇

b)   10-12 points   =   Raise 1♣/1◇ to 3♣/3◇

c)   13-15 points   =   Bid another 4-card suit or 3NT in preference to a bid of 4♣ or 4◇

HOT TIP

Remember that hands with minor-suit fits generally play better in a No Trump contract unless particularly distributional. Also, if you are going to attempt a game contract, it will usually be easier to make nine tricks in 3NT than eleven in a minor suit.

EXAMPLE HANDS: Partner opens 1♣. What do you respond?

♠ 543	♠ KQJ3	♠ 42	♠ K5	♠ K54
♡ 765	♡ 543	♡ A64	♡ J987	♡ 43
♢ 654	♢ 32	♢ Q98	♢ Q32	♢ K543
♣ KQJ2	♣ J765	♣ KQ432	♣ AQ32	♣ AKJ8
6 HCP	7 HCP	11 HCP	12 HCP	14 HCP
2♣	1♠	3♣	1♡	1♢

EXAMPLE HANDS: Partner opens 1♢. What do you respond?

♠ 864	♠ J654	♠ A4	♠ 982	♠ Q64
♡ 43	♡ 987	♡ A43	♡ 42	♡ KQ65
♢ KQ43	♢ AJ74	♢ KJ87	♢ KQJ6	♢ A432
♣ Q543	♣ K7	♣ 5432	♣ AKJ2	♣ A4
7 HCP	9 HCP	12 HCP	14 HCP	15 HCP
2♢	1♠	3♢	2♣	1♡

CONTINUATIONS BY OPENER

The bouncing ball is once again back in opener's court. This time, however, the discovery of a minor-suit fit is not likely to get you quite as excited. So, with those wise words of wisdom from the last Hot Tip firmly implanted, remember to consider 3NT as a contract in preference to a game at the five level.

YOUR OPTIONS AFTER A RAISE TO THE TWO LEVEL: (6-9 HCP)

1♣ - 2♣ - ?	1♢ - 2♢ - ?

1)   10-15 HCP   -   PASS

With no hope of a 25-point game take the money.

2)   16-18 HCP   -   MAKE AN INVITATIONAL NOISE!

With a balanced hand try 2NT showing 17-18 HCP. Experience suggests that balanced hands with only 16 HCP should pass. With a non-balanced hand in the 16-18 HCP zone try bidding your second suit if you have one (forcing for one round) or rebid your own suit with six or more of them. Partner should be going to game with 8 or 9 HCP.

3)   19 HCP   -   BID GAME

Prefer a 3NT game when your hand is reasonably balanced. With an unsuitable shape show another suit (forcing as above) and await developments.

YOUR OPTIONS AFTER A RAISE TO THE THREE LEVEL: (10-12 HCP)

1♣ - 3♣ - ?	1◊ - 3◊ - ?

1)   13 or less HCP   -   PASS

Same message as before. Opposite an average of 11 HCP it is generally best policy to PASS and take the plus score.

2)   14+ HCP   -   BID GAME/CHANGE THE SUIT

Holding as few as 14 HCP should still tempt you to try 3NT for the game bonus – if you have a relatively balanced hand. Space is limited for detailed exploration though it is worth remembering that partner is unlikely to have a 4-card major.

3)   19 HCP   -   CONSIDER SLAM PROSPECTS

With a minimum of 29 HCP slam prospects are good.

EXAMPLE HANDS: Make your rebid as opener after 1♣ - 2♣ - ?

♠ K6	♠ AQ7	♠ KJ76	♠ KJ8	♠ A6
♡ AKJ7	♡ 53	♡ K4	♡ AQ6	♡ KQ9
◇ 62	◇ J6	◇ 65	◇ KQ4	◇ KJ3
♣ J8543	♣ AQJ973	♣ AKQ32	♣ QJ87	♣ KQJ87
12 HCP	14 HCP	16 HCP	18 HCP	19 HCP
Pass	Pass	2♠	2NT	3NT

EXAMPLE HANDS: Make your rebid as opener after 1◇ - 3◇ - ?

♠ AQ32	♠ K5	♠ KQ2	♠ 43	♠ KQ
♡ 4	♡ KJ65	♡ J76	♡ AKJ7	∨ J
◇ KJ8765	◇ A9743	◇ QJ765	◇ KQ864	◇ AJ876
♣ J7	♣ Q2	♣ AQ	♣ K6	♣ KQJ54
11 HCP	13 HCP	15 HCP	16 HCP	17 HCP
Pass	Pass	3NT	3♡	5◇

WITHOUT SUPPORT FOR PARTNER

(C) YOU CAN CHANGE THE SUIT

It has already been suggested that you should explore possible major-suit fits before supporting partner's minor. What do you do when you do not have support for either?

YOU CAN BID A NEW SUIT

A change of suit conceals an unlimited point count. Ranging from 6 HCP to a lot means that the bid is FORCING. Partner must reply and, therefore, you are guaranteed another bid.

In the interests of economy your new suit (usually your longest) should be called at the lowest possible level – regardless of your strength.

RULE

It is customary to reply with the cheapest suit holding two 4-card suits and the highest ranking suit with two 5-card suits.

If the rank of your suit precludes you from being able to bid it at the one level you are allowed to respond at the two level – providing you have at least 9 HCP. This does NOT mean you MUST respond at the two level as soon as you pick up 9 HCP!

HOT TIP

Whilst it is usual to reply in your longest suit first you should give priority to showing a major suit at the one level when holding 4-5 in a major/minor and less than 11 HCP when bidding your longest suit would force you to respond at the two level.

e.g.   ♠ Q765   ♡ 7   ◇ A76543   ♣ J5

Respond 1◇ to partner's opening bid of 1♣, but 1♠ is the correct response to an opening bid of 1♡.

EXAMPLE HANDS: Partner opens 1♣. What do you respond?

♠ A654	♠ 76	♠ KJ86	♠ QJ543	♠ AJ987
♡ J765	♡ A987	♡ KJ43	♡ K7654	♡ 432
◇ 654	◇ Q876	◇ 65	◇ A2	◇ AK87
♣ 32	♣ 654	♣ 987	♣ 7	♣ 3
5 HCP	6 HCP	8 HCP	10 HCP	12 HCP
Pass	1◇	1♡	1♠	1♠

EXAMPLE HANDS: Partner opens 1◇. What do you respond?

♠ Q976	♠ 86	♠ 7	♠ AJ65	♠ Q6
♡ 72	♡ KQ73	♡ A7532	♡ 32	♡ K6
◇ 973	◇ J765	◇ A832	◇ 87	◇ A432
♣ A432	♣ J43	♣ 972	♣ AQ543	♣ KQ862
6 HCP	7 HCP	8 HCP	11 HCP	14 HCP
1♠	1♡	1♡	2♣	2♣

EXAMPLE HANDS: Partner opens 1♡. What do you respond?

♠ J8532	♠ AK52	♠ QJ74	♠ 98765	♠ 32
♡ 7	♡ 972	♡ K82	♡ A6	♡ 2
◇ 654	◇ J65	◇ KJ865	◇ Q9	◇ AK987
♣ KJ73	♣ 842	♣ J	♣ KQ54	♣ AK987
5 HCP	8 HCP	11 HCP	11 HCP	14 HCP
Pass	1♠	2◇	1♠	2◇

EXAMPLE HANDS: Partner opens 1♠. What do you respond?

♠ 7	♠ K7	♠ 642	♠ A4	♠ 5
♡ K642	♡ 43	♡ KQ62	♡ KJ654	♡ Q8754
◇ J732	◇ A65	◇ AJ74	◇ Q32	◇ KQJ42
♣ J942	♣ Q87654	♣ 43	♣ J85	♣ AJ
5 HCP	9 HCP	10 HCP	11 HCP	13 HCP
Pass	2♣	2◇	2♡	2♡

RULE

Over 1♠ a response of 2♡ shows AT LEAST 5 hearts. Responses of 2♣ or 2◇, however, only promise 4-card suits.

(D) YOU CAN RESPOND IN NO TRUMPS

By now you are probably bursting to know what to bid with 6, 7 or 8 HCP, no support for partner and a suit that can't be mentioned at the one level! The answer is 1NT.

a) 6-9 HCP = Respond 1NT
(may contain a singleton or even a void)

b) 10-12 HCP = Respond 2NT

c) 13-15 HCP = Respond 3NT

Responding with a No Trump bid should generally be used as a last resort. Even if your hand is balanced there is no reason to presume that a No Trump contract will produce the best result. No Trumps can often be suggested later.

Your priority is always to bid an intervening suit – certainly before calling 1NT and often before jumping to 2NT or 3NT; i.e. in reply to an opening bid of 1♡ a response in No Trumps would deny holding four spades.

A response of 1NT may be unbalanced. This happens frequently when you are obliged to respond with 6, 7 or 8 HCP without being able to mention a suit at the one level.

Note that by responding 1NT to an opening bid of 1♣ you will deny ANY other 4-card suit. Ergo, your ONLY suit is clubs! As a response of 2♣ elicits a similar message it is desirable to create a different point range to distinguish between the two types of hand. Use a response of 1NT here to show 8-10 HCP.

EXAMPLE HANDS: Partner opens 1♣. What do you respond?

♠ J654	♠ J43	♠ 962	♠ K54	♠ AJ7
♡ Q973	♡ 973	♡ J64	♡ A43	♡ Q52
◇ KJ62	◇ J43	◇ Q98	◇ J32	◇ K54
♣ 5	♣ AJ42	♣ KQ43	♣ A932	♣ KQ32
7 HCP	7 HCP	8 HCP	12 HCP	15 HCP
1◇	2♣	1NT	2NT	3NT

EXAMPLE HANDS: Partner opens 1◇. What do you respond?

♠ J75	♠ 54	♠ 864	♠ 982	♠ AQ4
♡ QJ7	♡ J7	♡ 954	♡ J64	♡ K65
◇ 862	◇ Q74	◇ KQ2	◇ 65	◇ Q73
♣ J942	♣ K97543	♣ QJ74	♣ AKJ54	♣ J987
5 HCP	6 HCP	8 HCP	9 HCP	12 HCP
Pass	1NT	1NT	2♣	2NT

EXAMPLE HANDS: Partner opens 1♡. What do you respond?

♠ A762	♠ 854	♠ KJ3	♠ KJ86	♠ AJ7
♡ 765	♡ A3	♡ 432	♡ 5	♡ J98
◊ 973	◊ KJ75	◊ QJ32	◊ AJ74	◊ QJ86
♣ Q32	♣ J863	♣ KJ7	♣ K864	♣ KJ9
6 HCP	9 HCP	11 HCP	12 HCP	13 HCP
1♠	1NT	2NT	1♠	3NT

EXAMPLE HANDS: Partner opens 1♠. What do you respond?

♠ 52	♠ 8	♠ K87	♠ 54	♠ J86
♡ KJ753	♡ 43	♡ 987	♡ J43	♡ AKQ3
◊ J54	◊ AJ752	◊ Q765	◊ QJ2	◊ J64
♣ J94	♣ J8654	♣ Q42	♣ A9743	♣ J72
6 HCP	6 HCP	7 HCP	8 HCP	12 HCP
1NT	1NT	1NT	1NT	2NT

Continuations by opener for (C) and (D) of this chapter are tackled in Chapters Four and Five.

HOT TIP

Holding exactly 9 HCP and a balanced hand you may have a choice between responding 1NT or choosing to bid a new suit at the two level. Prefer 1NT UNLESS you hold a 5-card suit.

HANDY HINTS

A change of suit at the ONE LEVEL shows 6+ HCP.

A non-jump change of suit at the TWO LEVEL shows 9+ HCP.

After a change of suit by responder, opener must make a rebid unless their right-hand opponent makes an intervening bid.

The auction 1♠ - 2♡ shows AT LEAST 5 hearts.

Always show intervening suits in preference to bidding No Trumps.

Chapter Four

REBIDS BY OPENER AFTER A SUIT OPENING BID

(A) BALANCED HANDS WITH 15-19 HCP

Logically enough balanced hands that are too strong to be opened 1NT are described with a rebid in No Trumps.

So, after opening the bidding with one of a suit, balanced hands in the 15-19 HCP range now need to be divided into smaller point bands.

Depending on whether your partner has responded at the ONE level or the TWO level will help direct you to the appropriate level for your own rebid.

RULE

Providing partner has not bid a 4-card major in which you also hold four cards you should proceed as originally planned, and rebid the appropriate number of No Trumps. Ergo, even if partner responds in a minor suit where you also hold four cards plod on with your No Trump rebid.

AFTER A ONE-LEVEL RESPONSE:

(Partner has shown 6+ HCP)

1NT	=	15-16 HCP
2NT	=	17-18 HCP
3NT	=	19 HCP

If you hold 15-16 HCP and partner responds 1NT to your suit opening bid you may feel a trifle put out as your intended rebid has now been stolen. The answer is to PASS. But, I hear you say, what if partner has 9 HCP and you have 16 HCP? Remember that partner would have preferred to reply with a new suit at the two level holding exactly 9 HCP and a 5-card suit. This means that if partner is sitting with a 9-point hand the distribution will be poor; either 4-3-3-3 or 4-4-3-2. Thus, the few occasions where you might miss playing in a successful 25-point game are now significantly reduced.

Note too sequences like 1◇ - 2◇ - 2NT and 1♠ - 2♠ - 3NT. The responder in both of these auctions may only have 6 HCP. Opener, therefore, passes with balanced hands holding 15-16 HCP and rebids 2NT and 3NT as if partner had replied at the one level.

RULE

A rebid of 2NT opposite a hand that may have as few as 6 HCP shows 17-18 HCP.

RULE

A rebid of 3NT opposite a hand that may have as few as 6 HCP shows 19 HCP.

AFTER A TWO-LEVEL RESPONSE:
(Partner has shown 9+ HCP)

2NT	=	15-16 HCP
3NT	=	17-19 HCP

Unable to make a rebid of 1NT after a two-level response means you must squash 17, 18 or 19 HCP into the one rebid of 3NT. No problem there.

Of course, you will have noticed that holding 16 HCP opposite a response at the two level guarantees you the combined magic 25 HCP required to attempt game. Agreed. While your limit-style rebid of 2NT can, theoretically, be passed let's put ourselves in partner's shoes for a moment. Partner, holding 9 HCP, is quite aware of your combined strength. Promoting a 9-point hand with a 5-card suit to a two-level response has automatically given it the power of a 10-point hand. Partner, therefore, will not leave you in 2NT. A conundrum for the uninitiated – sorry!

HOT TIP

Having spent the first three chapters drumming in the fact that you only need 25 points to attempt game does not mean that you will be successful every time. The art is to combine judgement with consistency. Experience proves that two balanced hands containing a combination of 25 HCP will frequently struggle without some of the qualities mentioned in the chapter on Hand Evaluation.

EXAMPLE HANDS: Select your rebid after 1♡ - 1♠

♠ KQ4	♠ J843	♠ J64	♠ KJ5	♠ KQ6
♡ KJ63	♡ AJ75	♡ Q9852	♡ AQJ3	♡ A432
◇ A32	◇ KJ7	◇ AQJ	◇ 87	◇ QJ73
♣ Q75	♣ KQ	♣ AQ	♣ KQJ2	♣ AK
15 HCP	15 HCP	16 HCP	17 HCP	19 HCP
1NT	2♠	1NT	2NT	3NT

Would you have rebid differently if partner had responded 1NT?

Pass	Pass	Pass	2NT	3NT

EXAMPLE HANDS: Select your rebid after 1♡ - 2♣

♠ AJ75	♠ Q4	♠ K72	♠ AK	♠ AKQ2
♡ K983	♡ KQ43	♡ J872	♡ Q862	♡ A973
◇ J5	◇ AJ5	◇ AKJ7	◇ QJ5	◇ Q32
♣ AQ8	♣ KJ72	♣ AJ	♣ AQ85	♣ KJ
15 HCP	16 HCP	17 HCP	18 HCP	19 HCP
2NT	2NT	3NT	3NT	3NT

(B) RESPONDER'S CONTINUATIONS

It seems appropriate at this point to discuss partner's continuations in reply to your descriptive, limited rebid.

In just the same way that the partner of a 1NT opening bid takes control of the auction – so it should happen here.

OPTIONS FOR RESPONDER AFTER;

(1) OPENER REBIDS 1NT WITH 15 OR 16 HCP
(a) PASS

With less than 9 HCP there is unlikely to be a play for game. Most balanced hands will be quite safe being played in a 1NT contract.

(b)   2♣ 2◇ 2♡ 2♠

Distributional hands with 6-8 HCP will probably generate more tricks if played in a trump suit. Be it a rebid in partner's suit, or your own suit or even a new suit (providing it is not a responder's reverse – see page 85) you are expressing a weak hand that requests partner to pass or give preference.

(c)   2NT

On the edge of a 25-point game if partner is maximum your response of 2NT promises exactly 9 HCP – accurately pin-pointing your combined strength. Partner will bid game with 16 HCP.

(d)   3♣ 3◇ 3♡ 3♠

A jump to the three level in a new suit or partner's opening bid suit creates a game-forcing auction, and shows a distributional hand with 9 or more HCP. By contrast, a jump rebid in your own suit is purely invitational – with a 6-card suit.

(e)   GAME BIDS

A limited sign-off based on information received.

EXAMPLE HANDS: Make your rebid as responder after 1◇ - 1♡ - 1NT - ?

♠ 73	♠ 86	♠ A752	♠ AJ5	♠ KQ3
♡ QJ8642	♡ AJ765	♡ KJ32	♡ J752	♡ A962
◇ QJ2	◇ 2	◇ 42	◇ Q43	◇ 65
♣ 42	♣ Q9753	♣ 842	♣ J92	♣ J842
6 HCP	7 HCP	8 HCP	9 HCP	10 HCP
2♡	2♣	Pass	2NT	3NT

EXAMPLE HANDS: Make your rebid as responder after 1♡ - 1♠ - 1NT - ?

♠ J8642	♠ KQJ7	♠ AKJ862	♠ KQ432	♠ QJ872
♡ 32	♡ A43	♡ 65	♡ K84	♡ A3
◇ KJ7	◇ 876	◇ K82	◇ 76	◇ KJ76
♣ J82	♣ 752	♣ 65	♣ K72	♣ J2
6 HCP	10 HCP	11 HCP	11 HCP	12 HCP
Pass	3NT	4♠	3♡	3◇

EXAMPLE HANDS: Make your rebid as responder after 1♣ - 1◊ - 1NT - ?

♠ A862	♠ Q54	♠ QJ7	♠ A832	♠ 32
♡ J972	♡ Q3	♡ KQ32	♡ 86	♡ K3
◊ Q652	◊ KJ9876	◊ J987	◊ K8642	◊ AQ654
♣ 9	♣ J7	♣ 54	♣ AJ	♣ KJ72
7 HCP	9 HCP	9 HCP	12 HCP	13 HCP
Pass	3◊	2NT	3NT	3♣

EXAMPLE HANDS: Make your rebid as responder after 1◊ - 1♠ - 1NT - ?

♠ QJ9876	♠ J742	♠ AJ97654	♠ A432	♠ KQJ85
♡ K64	♡ Q2	♡ 7	♡ 87	♡ AK72
◊ Q32	◊ Q2	◊ J8	◊ J862	◊ 75
♣ J	♣ A6542	♣ QJ2	♣ KQJ	♣ 92
9 HCP	9 HCP	9 HCP	11 HCP	13 HCP
3♠	2NT	4♠	3NT	3♡

(2) OPENER REBIDS 2NT WITH 15 OR 16 HCP
OPENER REBIDS 2NT WITH 17 OR 18 HCP

(a) PASS

With little space to explore if your hand has a borderline decision your judgement will often be the critical factor in determining your fate! In response to a jump rebid of 2NT you will likely-as-not pass with 6 or 7 HCP and go to game with 8 or more. If you have already responded at the two level it is rare to pass — if at all.

(b) 3♣ 3◊ 3♡ 3♠

If you are rebidding your own suit the message is one of weakness with fears that game will be a tall order. Whilst technically non-forcing, opener should sensibly assess game prospects. If, however, the suit you call is new or belongs to partner the bid is forcing to at least game.

(c) GAME BIDS

A limited sign-off based on information received.

EXAMPLE HANDS: Make your rebid as responder after 1♣ - 1♠ - 2NT - ?

♠ K642	♠ QJ8765	♠ AQ8765	♠ KQJ76	♠ AK72
♡ 876	♡ Q53	♡ K87	♡ QJ754	♡ Q7
◇ QJ2	◇ J87	◇ 54	◇ 4	◇ Q65
♣ 765	♣ 5	♣ 32	♣ J4	♣ 8752
6 HCP	6 HCP	9 HCP	10 HCP	11 HCP
Pass	3♠	4♠	4♡	3NT

EXAMPLE HANDS: Make your rebid as responder after 1♡ - 2◇ - 2NT - ?

♠ 654	♠ AQ7	♠ K9752	♠ 2	♠ A5
♡ A3	♡ K42	♡ 5	♡ Q3	♡ 73
◇ KJ765	◇ J8752	◇ AQ7532	◇ KQJ8765	◇ KQ764
♣ J53	♣ 32	♣ J	♣ K87	♣ KQ32
9 HCP	10 HCP	10 HCP	11 HCP	14 HCP
3NT	3♡	3♠	5◇	3♣

(3) OPENER REBIDS 3NT WITH 19 HCP
OPENER REBIDS 3NT WITH 17, 18 OR 19 HCP

Although game has already been reached there are still plenty of options available to responder. After all just because one hand is balanced it does not mean that 3NT is the best contract. There may be slam possibilities too. Needless to say, all bids over 3NT are forcing to a game or slam.

EXAMPLE HANDS: Make your rebid as responder after 1◇ - 1♡ - 3NT - ?

♠ Q2	♠ 62	♠ J82	♠ KJ65	♠ 3
♡ KJ85	♡ KQJ876	♡ AQJ72	♡ A432	♡ AK862
◇ 876	◇ 53	◇ 742	◇ 4	◇ AJ82
♣ 8765	♣ 752	♣ 75	♣ QJ82	♣ Q32
6 HCP	6 HCP	8 HCP	11 HCP	14 HCP
Pass	4♡	Pass	Pass	4◇

EXAMPLE HANDS: Make your rebid as responder after 1♠ - 2♣ - 3NT - ?

♠ 54	♠ J82	♠ K8	♠ 2	♠ AJ8
♡ AQ432	♡ KJ43	♡ 2	♡ K862	♡ A85
◇ -	◇ 32	◇ Q32	◇ KQ92	◇ K2
♣ KJ9876	♣ AQ53	♣ AQ87654	♣ QJ82	♣ 98762
10 HCP	11 HCP	11 HCP	11 HCP	12 HCP
4♡	Pass	4♣	Pass	Pass

Hands with slam potential need further clarification. The information you need will be revealed as you progress through this book.

HOT TIP SUMMARY TABLE FOR NO TRUMP REBIDS	
OPENER'S REBID	RESPONDER'S REBID
1NT Rebid = 15-16 HCP After a one-level response	Pass or weak takeout at two level with 6-8 HCP. Invite to game with 9 HCP. Bid 2NT or jump in own 6-card suit. Bid game with 10+ HCP or jump in new or partner's suit.
2NT Rebid = 15-16 HCP After a two-level response	Rebid of own suit = non-forcing. All other bids forcing to at least game with 9+ HCP.
2NT Rebid = 17-18 HCP After a one-level response	Rebid of own suit = non-forcing. All other bids forcing to at least game with 8+ HCP.
3NT Rebid = 19 HCP After a one-level response 3NT Rebid = 17-19 HCP After a two-level response	Pass if balanced and/or no slam interest. Correct to game in your major suit with 6+ cards. Bid new suit with extra shape and/or slam interest.

Chapter Five

REBIDS BY OPENER AFTER A SUIT OPENING BID

... and partner has not supported your suit.

(A) UNBALANCED HANDS WITH 10-19 HCP

Unsuitable for an immediate rebid in No Trumps non-balanced hands need to explore other avenues first. Your expedition will hopefully give partner a perfect picture of your shape. By offering a second suit you will be describing a minimum of 5-4 in distribution. Partner may well be relieved to be given a choice of trump suits. A rebid of opener's suit frequently infers a 6-carder. Of course it's not quite that simple! There will be a BARRIER for you to cross ...

Unbalanced hands conceal a much wider point-range than those in the balanced zone. From a distributional hand containing a meagre 10 HCP right up to 19 or even 20 HCP the net is wide – but, for responder, catching the ball is not always easy!

Having opened the bidding with one of a suit your next call will be a rebid of either:

☺ PARTNER'S SUIT

☺ YOUR SUIT

☺ A NEW SUIT

Leaving aside the problematic 4-4-4-1 shapes, two-suited hands which are non-balanced will always contain at least a 5-4 distribution. This pattern is important for the responder to visualise. It is the key to locating 5-3 fits. Similarly, when opener's rebid guarantees a 6-card suit responder should be content to support with as few as 2 cards.

Opener has two tasks to perform; (a) to show the shape of the hand and (b) the strength.

Setting the scene; You have opened the bidding. Partner has made a SIMPLE RESPONSE (i.e. has not jumped the bidding) in a new suit or bid 1NT. The ball is back in your court ...

Opener's hand is divided into three point bands:

(A) HANDS IN THE 10-15 HCP ZONE – (SMALL)

1) Support partner with 4 cards at the lowest level.   1♡-1♠-2♠

2) Rebid your suit with 5+ cards at the lowest level.   1◇-1♠-2◇

3) Bid a new suit below 2 of the suit you opened.   1♡-1♠-2◇

(B) HANDS IN THE 16-18 HCP ZONE – (MEDIUM)

1) Jump raise responder's suit with 4-card support.   1◇-1♠-3♠

2) Make a jump rebid in your own suit with 6+ cards.   1♡-1♠-3♡

3) Bid a new suit below 2 of the suit you opened.   1♡-1♠-2♣

4) Bid a new suit above 2 of the suit you opened.   1♣-1♠-2♡

5) Jump in a new suit after a 2-level response.   1♡-2♣-3◇

(C) HANDS IN THE 19(20) HCP ZONE – (LARGE)

1) Bid game in partner's major with 4+ card support.   1♡-1♠-4♠

2) Jump raise partner's minor to the 4 level.   1♠-2♣-4♣

3) Jump to game in own suit (6+ cards).   1♡-1♠-4♡

4) Make a jump rebid in your own suit after a 2-level
   response (6+ cards).   1♡-2♣-3♡

5) Bid a new suit above 2 of the suit you opened.   1♣-1♠-2◇

6) Jump in a new suit.   1♡-1♠-3♣

Quite a lot to absorb in one go!
(and yes, there are some overlaps – not misprints!)

Not forgetting that responder's change of suit is forcing, with an unlimited point count, it is impossible, as yet, to ascertain your side's combined strength. The best you can do, for now, is to give partner at least some indication of where you live. So, tell partner how big your house is!

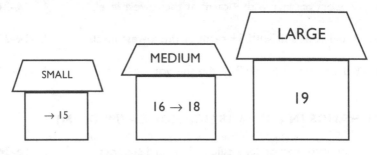

☺   **SUPPORT PARTNER'S SUIT:**

1◇ - 1♠ 2♠	Single raise Up to 15 points SMALL HAND	A single raise after a one-level response shows a weak hand with 4+ card support
1♡ - 2◇ 3◇	Single raise Up to 15 points SMALL HAND	A single raise after a two-level response shows a weak hand with 4+ card support (*)
1♣ - 1♡ 3♡	Double raise 16-18 points MEDIUM HAND	A double raise of a major or minor suit introduced at the one level is invitational with 16-18 HCP and 4+ card support
1♠ - 2♣ 4♣	Double raise of a minor suit MEDIUM/LARGE	A double raise of a minor after a two-level response is game-forcing with 4+ card support
1◇ - 1♠ 4♠	Game raise 19 points LARGE HAND	A game raise after a one-level response shows 19 HCP and 4+ card support
1♠ - 2♡ 4♡	Game raise 16-19 points MEDIUM/LARGE	A game raise after a two-level response shows 16-19 HCP and 4+ card support (*)

(*) 1♠ - 2♡ - 3♡/4♡ promises 3+ card support

EXAMPLE HANDS: Make your rebid as opener after 1♡ - 1♠ - ?

♠ AJ43	♠ KQ65	♠ AK74	♠ QJ32	♠ AQJ7
♡ QJ876	♡ AK876	♡ KJ543	♡ KQ76	♡ Q9753
◊ K74	◊ J6	◊ 3	◊ A86	◊ AK
♣ 4	♣ 32	♣ KQ5	♣ AJ	♣ K5
11 HCP	13 HCP	16 HCP	17 HCP	19 HCP
2♠	2♠	3♠	3♠	4♠
small	small	medium	medium	large

EXAMPLE HANDS: Make your rebid as opener after 1♠ - 2♣ - ?

♠ A87654	♠ QJ754	♠ AQ654	♠ AKQ32	♠ AKJ82
♡ 3	♡ K87	♡ KJ	♡ 8	♡ A3
◊ 76	◊ 2	◊ J9	◊ K83	◊ A3
♣ KQJ7	♣ AQ43	♣ KQ53	♣ AJ87	♣ K876
10 HCP	12 HCP	16 HCP	17 HCP	19 HCP
3♣	3♣	4♣	4♣	4♣
small	small	medium	medium	large

EXAMPLE HANDS: Make your rebid as opener after 1◊ - 1♡ - ?

♠ 6	♠ KQ2	♠ KJ	♠ K2	♠ AJ
♡ J972	♡ KJ53	♡ KJ32	♡ AQ32	♡ AK82
◊ AK543	◊ AJ862	◊ KQJ76	◊ AJ962	◊ KQ765
♣ K52	♣ Q	♣ Q2	♣ QJ	♣ Q2
11 HCP	16 HCP	16 HCP	17 HCP	19 HCP
2♡	3♡	3♡	3♡	4♡
small	medium	medium	medium	large

> ## HOT TIP
>
> Remember that the exception to rebidding No Trumps with balanced hands is when you have located a major-suit fit. Hence the exception to promising a 5-4 distribution! (e.g. 1♡-1♠-2♠)

RESPONDER'S CONTINUATIONS

1◇ - 1♠ 2♣ - Pass	6-9	HCP	Pass. Opposite a SMALL hand game is unlikely.
1◇ - 1♠ 2♣ - 3♣	10-12	HCP	An invitation to game if opener is MAXIMUM i.e. 14 or 15 HCP.
1◇ - 1♠ 2♣ - 4♣	13+	HCP	Responder can guarantee 25 HCP.
1♡ - 2◇ 3◇ - 3NT	11+	HCP	No room to invite, so have a go for game with 11+ HCP.
1♠ - 2♣ 4♣ - 5♣	9+	HCP	4♣ forced you to pick a game or slam in ♣ or ♠.
1♣ - 1♡ 3♡ - Pass	6-7	HCP	Pass as 25 HCP is unlikely.
1♣ - 1♡ 4♡ - Pass	6+	HCP	Game reached. Responder passes unless a slam looks possible.
1♣ - 1♡ 3♡ - 4♡	8+	HCP	Bid game as 25 HCP is likely.

Remember we need 25 points for game.

☺   REBID YOUR OWN SUIT:

Without support for partner you will either have to rebid the suit you opened or bid a new suit. This section will give you examples of single-suited hands.

EXAMPLE HANDS: Make your rebid as opener after 1♡ - 1♠ - ?

♠ 4	♠ K3	♠ A5	♠ QJ	♠ Q2
♡ AK7654	♡ AKQJ6	♡ KQJ654	♡ AQ6543	♡ AQ97654
◇ A76	◇ 872	◇ K6	◇ AQJ	◇ AQ
♣ 543	♣ J32	♣ KJ6	♣ Q2	♣ KQ
11 HCP	14 HCP	17 HCP	18 HCP	19 HCP
2♡	2♡	3♡	3♡	4♡
small	small	medium	medium	large

EXAMPLE HANDS: Make your rebid as opener after 1♠ - 2◇ - ?

♠ KQJ7543	♠ AQ5432	♠ KJ9876	♠ AKQ643	♠ KQJ987
♡ A65	♡ 3	♡ AQ5	♡ KJ	♡ AJ
◇ 76	◇ KQ5	◇ AJ8	◇ 32	◇ KQ2
♣ 9	♣ Q42	♣ J	♣ A86	♣ QJ
10 HCP	13 HCP	16 HCP	17 HCP	19 HCP
2♠	2♠	3♠	3♠	3♠
small	small	medium	medium	large

RULE

A jump rebid in your own suit guarantees at least a 6-card suit. A simple rebid of the suit you opened may be made with as few as 5, unless partner has responded in No Trumps when 6 are preferable.

☺   REBID A NEW SUIT:

By far the most complex section houses hand types which are two-suited without support for partner. In other words you want to introduce a 3rd suit. (This includes a 1NT response as a second suit).

Picture an imaginary BARRIER of TWO OF THE SUIT THAT YOU HAVE OPENED and you are half way to solving the mystery of the two-suited nightmare!

OPEN	1♣	AND YOUR BARRIER IS	2♣
OPEN	1◇	AND YOUR BARRIER IS	2◇
OPEN	1♡	AND YOUR BARRIER IS	2♡
OPEN	1♠	AND YOUR BARRIER IS	2♠

RULE

The barrier is ALWAYS two of the suit that you have opened. If you rebid a THIRD suit ABOVE the barrier you have REVERSED.

RULE

To break the barrier (or reverse) you guarantee a minimum of 16 HCP. This does not mean that you CAN always break the barrier with 16! Some hands require 19 HCP after a one-level response! ☹

AFTER A TWO-LEVEL RESPONSE – which promises at least 9 HCP
With a SMALL hand (10-15 HCP) you cannot cross the barrier. Suits can be bid up to and including a rebid of two of the barrier suit.

With a MEDIUM (16-18 HCP) or LARGE (19 HCP) hand you MUST cross the barrier. Get over it quickly and economically!

Holding 16 or more HCP you are now in possession of information regarding definite game prospects and possible slam hopes. By REVERSING and crossing the BARRIER you can let partner know too!

EXAMPLE HANDS: Make your rebid as opener after 1♡ - 2♣ - ?

♠ A843	♠ 76	♠ KQ65	♠ K94	♠ AQ74
♡ KJ876	♡ KQ432	♡ AQ874	♡ AKQJ5	♡ KQJ53
◇ A43	◇ AKQ2	◇ J9	◇ K864	◇ J6
♣ 4	♣ 43	♣ KJ	♣ 3	♣ AQ
12 HCP	14 HCP	16 HCP	16 HCP	19 HCP
2♡	2◇	2♠	3◇	2♠
small	small	medium REVERSE	medium REVERSE	large REVERSE

EXAMPLE HANDS: Make your rebid as opener after 1♠ - 2◇ - ?

♠ KQJ52	♠ AJ875	♠ K7654	♠ AKJ86	♠ AQJ75
♡ KQ98	♡ AKJ7	♡ KQ3	♡ AJ65	♡ 4
◇ 765	◇ 43	◇ 3	◇ A32	◇ Q43
♣ 2	♣ Q4	♣ AKJ5	♣ 4	♣ AKQJ
11 HCP	15 HCP	16 HCP	17 HCP	19 HCP
2♡	2♡	3♣	3♡	3♣
small	small	medium REVERSE	medium REVERSE	large REVERSE

AFTER A ONE-LEVEL RESPONSE – which promises only 6 HCP
With a SMALL hand (10-15 HCP) you cannot cross the barrier. Suits can be bid up to and including a rebid of the barrier suit.

With a MEDIUM hand (16-18 HCP) you may only cross the barrier if you can do so WITHOUT JUMPING THE BIDDING. Your reverse here shows 16+ HCP (i.e. includes a LARGE hand with 19 HCP too) and is forcing for one round only.

If you are forced to jump the bidding in order to get over the barrier, you create a GAME FORCING auction. Opposite a hand that may contain as few as 6 HCP this would be folly unless you held 19 HCP. Therefore, you may only do this with a LARGE hand.

Just to recap, a rebid of a new suit BELOW the barrier in reply to a one-level response describes a hand that may be SMALL or MEDIUM if a reverse would have required a jump bid.

LARGE hands MUST cross the barrier immediately to express their strength. Failure to do this would deny 19 HCP.

RULE

If you rebid a new suit BELOW the barrier your bid is NOT FORCING.

RULE

Reverses after a two-level response are FORCING TO GAME.

RULE

Reverses made via a JUMP BID (perforce) are FORCING TO GAME.

RULE

A simple reverse after a one-level response is only FORCING FOR ONE ROUND.

EXAMPLE HANDS: Make your rebid as opener after 1◇ - 1♠ - ?

♠ 9	♠ A7	♠ K3	♠ KJ	♠ KQ3
♡ AKQ2	♡ 9	♡ AQ82	♡ K	♡ QJ98
◇ K8765	◇ AQ9876	◇ J9876	◇ KQJ42	◇ AKQJ2
♣ 432	♣ KJ76	♣ AK	♣ KQJ32	♣ J
12 HCP	14 HCP	17 HCP	19 HCP	19 HCP
2◇	2♣	2♡	3♣	2♡
small	small	medium	large	large
		REVERSE	REVERSE	REVERSE

EXAMPLE HANDS: Make your rebid as opener after 1♡ - 1NT - ?

♠ K654	♠ AJ75	♠ AK85	♠ Q8	♠ KQJ2
♡ QJ765	♡ KQ8763	♡ AQ865	♡ AKQ76	♡ KQJ87
◇ K4	◇ J	◇ QJ7	◇ 97	◇ A2
♣ A2	♣ K4	♣ 4	♣ AKJ5	♣ K3
13 HCP	14 HCP	16 HCP	19 HCP	19 HCP
Pass	2♡	2♠	3♣	2♠
small	small	medium REVERSE	large REVERSE	large REVERSE

EXAMPLE HANDS: Make your rebid as opener after 1◇ - 1♡ - ?

♠ A4	♠ AJ83	♠ K93	♠ AKQ2	♠ A
♡ Q3	♡ K8	♡ 4	♡ 86	♡ K3
◇ KQ854	◇ AQJ87	◇ AKQ32	◇ AKJ62	◇ AQ6542
♣ J543	♣ J6	♣ KJ87	♣ Q6	♣ AQ43
12 HCP	16 HCP	16 HCP	19 HCP	19 HCP
2♣	1♠	2♣	2♠	3♣
small	medium	medium	large REVERSE	large REVERSE

EXAMPLE HANDS: Make your rebid as opener after 1♣ - 1♠ - ?

♠ J6	♠ 5	♠ AQ6	♠ AQJ	♠ 87
♡ AKQ3	♡ Q2	♡ KJ32	♡ -	♡ AJ75
◇ 54	◇ AKJ6	◇ 6	◇ KJ64	◇ AK
♣ Q9876	♣ A76542	♣ AQ875	♣ KQJ765	♣ AK876
12 HCP	14 HCP	16 HCP	17 HCP	19 HCP
2♣	2♣	2♡	2◇	2♡
small	small	medium REVERSE	medium REVERSE	large REVERSE

EXAMPLE HANDS: Make your rebid as opener after 1♣ - 1◊ - ?

♠ 62	♠ J876	♠ AKQ5	♠ 6	♠ AKJ75
♡ KQJ8	♡ A2	♡ 32	♡ KJ98	♡ AQ
◊ A2	◊ 4	◊ K8	◊ AQJ	◊ Q
♣ QJ752	♣ AKQ876	♣ AJ765	♣ AKJ92	♣ QJ973
13 HCP	14 HCP	17 HCP	19 HCP	19 HCP
1♡	1♠	1♠	2♡	2♠
small	small	medium	large REVERSE	large REVERSE

HOT TIP SUMMARY TABLE FOR REVERSING

THE BARRIER IS TWO OF THE SUIT OPENED

A rebid by opener in a new suit above the barrier constitutes a REVERSE

AFTER A ONE-LEVEL RESPONSE: (6+ HCP) (INCLUDING 1NT)

You may only reverse with 16-18 HCP if you can do so without jumping the bidding.

    eg   1◊ - 1♠ - 2♡

This reverse is forcing for one round only and shows 16+ HCP.

If a reverse bid forces you to make a jump bid you require 19 HCP.

    eg   1♣ - 1♡ - 2♠

This reverse is forcing to game.

Therefore, auctions which start 1♣ - 1♡ - 1♠ or 1♡ - 1♠ - 2♣ may conceal anywhere between 12-18 HCP in the opener's hand

AFTER A TWO-LEVEL RESPONSE: (9+ HCP)

You **must** reverse holding 16-19 HCP.

All reverses after a two-level response are forcing to game as the partnership is guaranteed a minimum of 25 HCP.

    eg   1♡ - 2♣ - 2♠

All reverses must be made as economically as possible

RULE

Always cross the barrier as economically as possible. i.e. NEVER JUMP THE BIDDING TO GET OVER THE BARRIER UNLESS IT IS THE ONLY WAY TO GET OVER IT!

HOT TIP

Whenever you are in a game-forcing auction there is never any rush to bid game! You can now explore at leisure and find out more information about each other's hand confident that your partner will not be passing below a game bid ... (famous last words).

HANDY HINTS

Do not make a jump rebid unless you have a strong hand.

Always raise partner's major with 4-card support.

Raise partner's minor with 4 unless you have an unbid major.

All reverses are forcing for a least one round.

A SIMPLE REVERSE after a one-level response shows 16+ HCP.

A FORCED JUMP REVERSE after a one-level response shows 19 HCP.

ALL REVERSES after a two-level response are forcing to game with 16+ HCP.

Chapter Six

DEVELOPMENT OF THE AUCTION

(A) RESPONDER'S REBID

Developing the auction is an art. Responder's rebid is frequently the last bastion in the midst of a battle. Indeed, it can also be claimed that this is the last piece of the jigsaw after a one-level opener!

Partner has opened the bidding with a suit. You have changed the suit. Partner has made a rebid and it's back to you. Perhaps partner's last call answered your prayers and you know which direction to take. If this is the case breathe a sigh of relief and get on with it.

More frequently, however, there is still an element of doubt about the final contract. Maybe this is because you have yet to discover a fit or perhaps your combined strength is still an unknown quantity. Now you find yourself in the dark, groping around for a descriptive rebid. Is it possible you should not even be bidding at all?

The development of the auction is in full swing only you don't know whether to press the accelerator or apply the brakes. It can be as exciting as it can be frustrating as it can be frightening. In the end, common sense should prevail. In the meantime, though, it's ...

TIME TO ASK YOURSELF SOME QUESTIONS

1.   Are you in a forcing auction or can you pass?

2.   Was partner's last bid invitational or a sign-off?

3.   Have you sufficient information to make a final decision?

4.   Have you already bid the full value of your hand within the context of the auction?

5.   Has the auction limited your combined strength or is there scope for adventure?

The list is endless but the most important consideration is;

WHAT EXACTLY DO YOU KNOW AT THIS POINT OF THE AUCTION?

Think about the distribution and strength of partner's hand. Look at your own.

1. Is there an obvious fit?

2. Do you have a known combined point range?

3. Should you be taking control or leaving it to partner?

4. Is there a bid that now adequately describes your hand?

5. Should you be passing?

Chapter Three introduced you to a section on limit bids for responder. Supporting partner or suggesting No Trumps at your first opportunity gave partner an accurate description of your limited hand and your contribution to the auction was over, for the most part.

Without the requirements for a limit bid, your first move, therefore, was to change the suit and explore. (6+ HCP if you replied at the one level or 9+ HCP if you made a simple response at the two level.)

Here is a reminder of partner's rebid options;

SUPPORT YOUR SUIT;   **REBID OWN SUIT;**
REBID NO TRUMPS;   **BID NEW SUIT;**

... and it's back to you.

While your first response did not categorise your point zone, at the end of the day you still live in a SMALL, MEDIUM, or LARGE house built for the responder! (Responder's who live in MANSIONS 16+ HCP need special help! See Chapter Nine.)

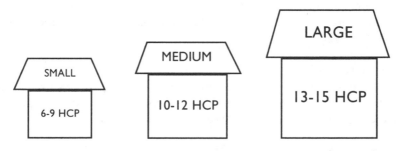

Armed with information you have since received, are you in a position to make a limit bid now?

MORE QUESTIONS FIRST ...

1. Is this the right contract?

2. Do you like the suggested "strain"?

3. Are you at the right level?

4. Is partner's rebid forcing?

Combine the answer to these questions with YOUR OPTIONS.

(A) PASS

(B) GIVE PREFERENCE TO ONE OF PARTNER'S SUITS

(C) RAISE ONE OF PARTNER'S SUITS

(D) REBID YOUR OWN SUIT

(E) REBID NO TRUMPS

(F) INTRODUCE A THIRD SUIT

(G) INTRODUCE THE FOURTH SUIT

Themes repeat themselves. Has partner shown a small, medium or large hand or, perhaps, a combination of two of them? Did partner reverse? If so, was it forcing for one round or forcing to game? You hold the key to your side's success. Will you take the money or open the box?

Here are some individual examples – with explanations – of the options available to you.

PASS OR PREFERENCE?
Strange as it may seem, when so much of our energy is channelled into locating an 8-card fit, there are times when you are reduced to supporting partner's possible 5-card suit with only 2! Let's see why.

♠	A765		
♡	J3		
◇	J82		
♣	Q765	1♡ - 1♠ - 2◇ - ?	small or medium

Faced with the prospect of playing in a 7-card trump fit – be it hearts or diamonds – does it matter which? There are three key factors to take into account here. Firstly, 5-2 fits are generally more successful as a trump suit than 4-3 combinations. Secondly, a making major-suit contract scores more than a minor-suit effort.

Most importantly, let's not forget that partner may be concealing as many as 18 HCP! Considering your total assets might reach 25 or 26 HCP it would be quite unacceptable to be languishing in a partscore. Partner might appreciate another chance to bid. On all three counts you should make a SIMPLE, albeit FALSE, PREFERENCE bid of 2♡. Partner will be aware that you may not actually like hearts. It merely shows that – all else being equal – you PREFER them to diamonds. Your rebid at the two level is still equivalent to the points shown by an initial raise – i.e. 6-9 HCP.

With a bit of luck this unpleasant option won't be the order of the day.

♠ J75	
♡ A752	
◇ K98	
♣ 432	1◇ - 1♡ - 2♣ - ? small or medium

More often than not you will hold 3-card support for partner's first-bid suit and it's problem solved. If you are fortunate enough to have been dealt three cards in both of partner's suits you must remember to give preference to the combined length rather than strength. Switch the minor suits around here and it is still correct to give preference with 2◇ – at the same time limiting your hand to the 6-9 HCP zone.

Preference can also be shown, of course, by passing. Giving up any hope of reaching game you are expressing a combination of weakness with a good reason for leaving partner to fester in their second suit. Given that you would strain to give partner a lift back to their first suit holding a 2-3 distribution in the two suits, you will generally only prefer to play in the second choice when you are either lucky enough to have 4-card support or your shape in those suits is 1-3.

♠ J7543	
♡ 6	
◇ KJ43	
♣ J63	1♡ - 1♠ - 2♣ - ? small or medium

If you think that bidding your spades again or introducing the diamond suit look like attractive alternatives to the 7-card club fit – think again. With partner having described the whereabouts of nine of their cards, imagine the possible distribution of the other four. Second-guessing your best fit is not likely to be productive. Better the devil you know … PASS!

♠   954
♥   Q432
♦   J76
♣   K32   1♣ - 1♥ - 2♦ - ?   medium or large

Did you recognise the reverse? The 2♦ rebid showed 16+ HCP as the new suit was introduced above two of the suit which had been opened. A reverse is forcing so you must bid – despite holding only 6 HCP. Fortunately, a preference bid of 3♣ is no hardship here. Not only do you genuinely prefer clubs as a trump suit your response was made at the lowest available level, expressing a weak hand with no desire to play in game unless partner is better than a minimum.

♠   J7654
♥   QJ32
♦   Q7
♣   K3   1♣ - 1♠ - 2♥ - ?   medium or large

Hooray! An 8-card major-suit fit and enough points to bid game even if partner only has a meagre 16. With only 6 or 7 HCP a bid of 3♥ would have sufficed but with your extra strength you have to take control and bid 4♥!

♠   K432
♥   J82
♦   Q432
♣   92   1♥ - 1♠ - 3♣ - ?   large

Another reverse but this time the jump over the barrier creates a game force. You do not have to bid game straight away, but with no slam ambition even opposite the equivalent of 19 HCP there's no point in deliberating. A jump to 4♥ indicates three trumps and relative weakness. With more points you can temporise with bidding just 3♥ – leaving room to explore for a possible slam.

HOT TIP

Bids which ear-mark an unlimited combined point count during a game-forcing auction suggest either an uncertainty about the strain in which to play or the correct level.

THEREFORE ...
'Fast arrival' to a game contract in a game-forcing auction expresses a limited hand in context. A slow exploratory auction, by contrast, leaves space for accuracy when unsure of the final contract.

The most important aspect, though, is recognising that if game has not yet been reached the auction must continue until it does.

Hands in the 6-9 HCP zone have limited options on their second turn to call in reply to a non-forcing rebid by opener, whereas hands with 10-12 HCP have game interest opposite as few as 14 HCP. This additional high-card strength creates opportunities to explore higher territory more safely. Whatever else happens you will not have to make an uncomfortable 'false' preference bid!

RAISE ONE OF PARTNER'S SUITS
Whether partner has introduced a new suit or rebid the same suit a picture of an unbalanced hand is painted.

♠ KJ876		
♡ 2		
◇ AJ72		
♣ Q62	1♡ - 1♠ - 2◇ - ?	small or medium

Following your change of suit, partner has now indicated a distributional hand with at least a 5-4 shape, also denying 4-card spade support. With partner holding anything up to 18 HCP opposite there are great chances of game. Keep the auction alive with a raise to 3◇. The message is twofold: not only do you promise 'primary' support for the second suit – which may only be a four-carder, but also your range is pinned down to 10-12 HCP – as if the bidding had started 1◇ - 3◇.

> **RULE**
>
> Raising a second suit – where only 4 cards are so-far guaranteed promises 4 of them too!

♠ QJ87
♡ 987
♢ KJ4
♣ A32   1♡ - 1♠ - 2♢ - ?   small or medium

Same auction as before but the rebid is entirely different. Facing a 5-card heart suit you have an obvious choice of calls. A jump raise to 3♡ gives partner the good news about your 3-card support together with game invitational values – i.e. 10-12 HCP. Add a couple of points and a game rebid of 4♡ would sum up your hand to perfection.

> **RULE**
>
> JUMP PREFERENCE guarantees an 8-card trump fit.

♠ J765
♡ K87
♢ 32
♣ A654   1♡ - 1♠ - 2NT - ?   17-18 bal

Modify the auction and once again the right answer is 3♡. This might look a trifle odd as the 2NT bidder has not promised a 5-card suit. But, partner MAY have five hearts concealed in that balanced rebid and a heart game may prove more successful than a shot at 3NT. The least you can do is consult partner with what is called 'delayed support' thereby offering partner a choice of games.

♠ 9876
♡ J3
♢ KJ4
♣ QJ32   1♡ - 1♠ - 3♡ - ?   medium

With a guaranteed 8-card heart fit your rebid is clearly 4♡. Although a No Trump game may superficially look to be a good prospect your spade holding might prove an embarrassment and scupper that idea.

> **RULE**
>
> Opposite a hand limited to 16-18 HCP and a 6- or 7-card suit you should have a reasonably good indication of your side's potential. Always attempt game with 8 or more HCP.

If your first response was 1NT showing 6-9 HCP, you are permitted, indeed, encouraged, to raise one of partner's suits with a known 8-card fit and the top end of your range i.e. 8 or 9 HCP. This not only gives partner the chance to continue the auction with a medium-strength hand (16-18 HCP), but also allows partner to assess game prospects even with a 'small' hand.

♠ AJ6
♡ 654
◇ KJ7
♣ 9876   1♠ - 1NT - 2◇ - ?   small or medium

With a concentration of high cards in partner's two suits your values are working 'overtime'. Give partner the good news with a jump to 3♠. A feeble preference bid of 2♠ would have seen you festering in a partscore opposite something like:

♠ KQ987
♡ 2
◇ AQ543
♣ J5

♠ 43
♡ J765
◇ K76
♣ KQ98   1♠ - 1NT - 2♣ - ?   small or medium

With such good clubs and a maximum there is undoubtedly scope for a game in No Trumps opposite a medium hand. e.g.:

♠ KQJ52
♡ KQ
◇ QJ
♣ A765

So let partner decide the next move over your descriptive rebid of 3♣. A lazy pass on either of these last examples would have been a waste of two possible opportunities for a game bonus.

> ### RULE
>
> Holding a hand known by partner to be limited to 6-9 HCP you should exercise judgement when you have a suitable maximum by giving preference at the three level.

REBID YOUR OWN SUIT

With a dislike for partner's offering what's to stop you bidding your own suit again? If you have already been denied 4-card support, insisting on a moth-eaten 5-carder as a trump suit may be disastrous unless partner produces 3 of them for you. With few exceptions it is generally only safe to rebid your suit when you have at least six unless, of course, your partner has already been good enough to support you. The level of your rebid – as always – will be determined by your strength.

♠ AQ8765
♡ 3
◇ 654
♣ 654   1♡ - 1♠ - 2♡ - ?   small

With no fit for partner and a good suit of your own a 2♠ rebid is clearly a sensible way to describe your assets. Opposite a 'small' hand with no second suit your choice of trump suit is likely to end the auction for your side. Partner should be under no illusion that your hand is any stronger than 6-9 HCP. With the same distribution and 10-12 HCP you would have selected a 3♠ rebid. Strong hands with 13+ HCP and a 6-card suit need to investigate further before leaping to game. This will be explained in more detail at the end of the chapter.

♠ AQ8765
♡ J54
◇ 654
♣ 3   1♡ - 1♠ - 2♣ - ?   small or medium

A trap hand! Tempting though it may be to show your spades again do not forget that partner has defined a 5-4 distribution. With an 8-card heart fit beckoning there is no reason to explore further. A 2♡ rebid expresses your 6-9 HCP hand to perfection.

♠ AJ876
♡ 2
◇ 54
♣ QJ765   1♡ - 1♠ - 2◇ - ?   small or medium

A typical situation where trouble may be looming. Misfitting hands can be dangerous. Keep cool and rebid 2♠. Don't try a rescue into 2NT as this will give partner the impression you have 10-12 HCP.

♠ 43
♡ AQJ543
◇ K8
♣ 654   1◇ - 1♡ - 1NT - ?   15-16 HCP

Facing a balanced hand it has to be safe to bid game in hearts. With a guaranteed 8 card major fit and at least 25 HCP there are no problems here. Change one of the hearts to a spade, however, and I would prefer a raise to 3NT.

If partner's rebid shows 4-card support for your suit the news will be more than welcome. Good news too when you also get to know the exact size of partner's house! With a discovered fit in a major your only task is to divine the correct level. Mercifully the goal posts will be in sight and, for the most part, your continuations were explained in Chapter Five.

♠ 765
♡ KJ65
◇ Q32
♣ 987   1◇ - 1♡ - 2♡ - ?   small

No obvious chance of game so stick.

♠ AK75
♡ KJ6
◇ 32
♣ 9852   1◇ - 1♠ - 2♠ - ?   small

Prospects have improved but game is only likely if partner is top of the range. Bid 3♠ and find out.

♠ J32
♡ J7652
◇ Q87
♣ Q3   1♣ - 1♡ - 3♡ - ?   medium

Alas we are bereft! Just a couple more points and you would have no hesitation in attempting game opposite a chunky 16-18 HCP.

If your supported suit was a minor there are other considerations. Perhaps nine tricks in a No Trump contract will prove easier to make than eleven in a minor suit contract. Perhaps you have delayed 3-card support for partner's original major suit which should be proffered in return as a potential trump suit. e.g.

♠ J87
♡ 32
◇ K63
♣ KQJ87   1♠ - 2♣ - 3♣ - ?   small

With 10-12 HCP and delayed support make a rebid of 3♠ and put the ball back in partner's court.

♠ K876
♡ A765
◇ Q765
♣ 3   1♣ - 1◇ - 2◇ - ?   small

Partner's small-hand rebid does not inspire us. Don't be persuaded to seek another spot. There is no major-suit fit and all the hallmarks of a plus score are right here. Pass!

REBID IN NO TRUMPS
In the absence of a fit for partner, or a good suit of your own, the contract sounds suitable for No Trump prospects. First, check to see if you have the essential requirements for this option. How big is your house? Are you in a position to rebid No Trumps at the appropriate level?

INT is still 6-9 HCP.
2NT is still 10-12 HCP.
3NT is still 13-15 HCP.

If you are considering a No Trump contract the opponents are likely to open their attack by leading the unbid suit. Therefore, after three suits have been mentioned, No Trumps should only be suggested holding a 'stop' – a minimum of Ax, Kx, Qxx or Jxxx – in the unbid suit.

♠ QJ2
♡ J54
◇ Q8654
♣ Q2   1♣ - 1◇ - 1♡ - ?   small or medium

INT denies primary support for hearts and, for the most part, is unlikely to have three cards in partner's minor. INT promises a stop in spades (the 4th suit) and 6-9 HCP. Perfect!

♠ AJ87
♡ 65
◇ KJ54
♣ 654   1♡ - 1♠ - 2♣ - ?   small or medium

The temptation to rebid 2NT should be resisted as this shows 10-12 HCP – just as if it had been bid a round earlier. Hands in the 6-9 HCP range, therefore, are denied this option and you are forced on these occasions to give preference to partner's offering or rebid your own suit. On this hand rebid 2♡. Add 1 HCP and 2NT is ideal. Give yourself an extra 4 HCP and a game rebid of 3NT would certainly fit the bill.

♠ AJ87
♡ 65
◇ KJ54
♣ 654   1♣ - 1◇ - 2♡ - ?   large

Did you recognise that game-forcing jump to get over the barrier in order to show a LARGE (19 HCP) hand? Your selection of high cards are appropriately placed to suggest a game in No Trumps and with no obvious sign of a slam your leap to 3NT – 'fast arrival' style – should convey this message.

♠ J76
♡ KQJ
◇ 32
♣ K8765   1◇ - 2♣ - 2♠ - ?   small or medium

Another reverse by partner tells us that once again we are in the game zone. Your strength in hearts will be most useful in a No Trump contract and this should be your first port of call. This is another opportunity to express your hand using the principle of 'fast arrival' which here shows a limited hand with top cards in the 4th suit.

Responder's options covered in this section to-date have one common theme; they are all able to describe limited hands within the context of the auction.

Your next and last two options are to introduce a new suit. It may be a 3rd suit or a 4th suit depending on the preceding auction. These two options have a similar property in that they conceal unlimited point zones. There is great depth to this area of the game where responder's rebid in a new suit is merely the prelude to the *denouement* of the auction. So, one more thing is sure; for simplicity I will only be touching the tip of the iceberg!

INTRODUCE A THIRD SUIT
Partner opens and rebids their own suit at simple level (i.e. without jumping the bidding) and it's over to you. Well, if you don't like what's on the menu you can always eat elswhere ...

RULE

A new suit BELOW two of the suit in which you first responded is NON-FORCING. Promising at least a 5-4 distribution you would like partner to choose one of YOUR suits.

♠ AQJ76
♡ Q7654
◇ 2
♣ 43   1◇ - 1♠ - 2◇ - ?   small

Your initial response has paved the way for an economically descriptive rebid. A 5-3 major-fit is not out of the question and on a good day you will find partner with four hearts. Issuing an invitation to give preference to one of your major suits at the two level is likely to net you the best chance of a plus score.

♠ 543
♡ KJ876
◇ KQ54
♣ 2   1♣ - 1♡ - 2♣ - ?   small

Another situation where you might try and improve the contract to date. There's plenty of room for partner to hold either three hearts or four diamonds.

RULE

A new suit ABOVE two of the suit in which you first responded is FORCING for at least one round and again suggests a minimum of 5-4 in distribution.

♠ 87
♡ AKJ8
◇ AJ765
♣ 65   1♣ - 1◇ - 2♣ - ?   small

A rebid of 2♡ is forcing for one round. Why? Because you have made a RESPONDER'S REVERSE! The 'Barrier' rule for reversing applies to responder as well as opener except you need only 11 HCP to cross it when used at the two level. You wouldn't be a very happy bunny if partner passed now, would you?!

♠ K765
♡ QJ642
◇ A5
♣ J5   1◇ - 1♡ - 2◇ - ?   small

Despite knowing there is no spade fit your rebid of 2♠ paints a pretty picture. Armed with the knowledge that you have a 5-4 pattern and 11 or more HCP partner will hopefully know where to land!

RULE

A new suit bid at the three level by either opener or responder is also shape-showing, but this time it is FORCING TO GAME!

♠ 2
♡ KJ876
◇ K754
♣ A65   1♠ - 2♡ - 2♠ - ?   small

If your reaction was to rebid 3◇ – think again! You are not strong enough to insist on game and this bid requires 13 or more HCP. You are left with a choice of 2NT or 2NT! Sorry – joke, no choice at all!

♠ K8765
♡ A2
◇ 43
♣ AKJ3   1◇ - 1♠ - 2◇ - ?   small

An instinctive 3♣ rebid is perfect here. Expecting you to have five spades, four clubs and 13+ HCP your partner will not be disappointed. The auction must continue until a game is reached.

EXAMPLE AUCTION: 1♠ - 2◇ - 2♠ (→ 15 HCP)   small
Make your rebid as responder having initially shown 9+ HCP.

♠ 43	♠ J6	♠ A87	♠ 5	♠ KQ2
♡ J76	♡ KQ76	♡ J32	♡ QJ98	♡ 43
◇ KQJ76	◇ QJ72	◇ AJ862	◇ KJ876	◇ AK862
♣ Q32	♣ K73	♣ 43	♣ AQ7	♣ J54
9 HCP	10-12 HCP	10-12 HCP	13-15 HCP	13-15 HCP
Pass	2NT	3♠	3NT	4♠

EXAMPLE AUCTION: 1♡ - 1♠ - 2♣ (→ 18 HCP)   small or medium
Make your rebid as responder having initially shown 6+ HCP.

♠ KJ9876	♠ K532	♠ Q6543	♠ J654	♠ AKJ876
♡ 2	♡ 543	♡ AJ7	♡ 76	♡ 43
◇ QJ7	◇ QJ87	◇ 32	◇ KQ32	◇ 96
♣ J72	♣ 65	♣ KJ7	♣ AQ3	♣ K32
6-9 HCP	6-9 HCP	10-12 HCP	10-12 HCP	10-12 HCP
2♠	2♡	3♡	2NT	3♠

EXAMPLE AUCTION: 1♡ - 1♠ - 2♣ (→ 18 HCP)   small or medium
Make your rebid as responder having initially shown 6+ HCP.

♠ J765	♠ A9653	♠ KJ76	♠ AKJ8	♠ KQJ65
♡ 876	♡ 5	♡ 32	♡ KJ8	♡ 53
◇ 543	◇ A76	◇ AJ98	◇ J764	◇ 765
♣ AQ3	♣ AQJ6	♣ KQ5	♣ 64	♣ AK4
6-9 HCP	13+ HCP	13-15 HCP	13-15 HCP	
2♡	4♣	3NT	4♡	???

OPENER GETS PREFERENCE BACK TO THEIR FIRST SUIT

Let's just go back to the scenario where opener held a two-suited hand with 16-18 HCP and was unable to make a rebid to highlight reversing values following a one-level response;

e.g. 1♡ - 1♠ - 2♣	=	small or medium
		(3♣ would show 19 HCP)
1♣ - 1♡ - 1♠	=	small or medium
		(2♠ would show 19 HCP)
1♠ - 1NT - 2◇	=	small or medium
		(3◇ would show 19 HCP)

Now we will assume that responder has indicated preference for the first bid suit at the two level, promising 6-9 HCP. What next? Having already described a 5-4 shape, the opener must continue with a bid that further describes his/her shape (not forgetting that the preference bid might have been made with only 2-card support).

e.g.   After 1♡ - 1♠ - 2♣ - 2♡:

3♡	=	6-4 in hearts and clubs
2♠	=	3-card spade support
2NT	=	Shows a stopper in diamonds
3♣	=	5-5 in hearts and clubs

Don't forget that all of these continuations show the medium range of 16-18 HCP since you would pass with less.

HOT TIP SUMMARY TABLE OF RESPONDER'S REBIDS

PASS OR PREFERENCE?

Following a simple rebid you can Pass or give simple preference at the TWO LEVEL which shows 6-9 HCP.

RAISE ONE OF PARTNER'S SUITS

Following a simple rebid you can raise partner's suit to the THREE LEVEL provided you can guarantee at least an 8-card fit. You need 10-12 HCP.*

* EXCEPTION – If your initial response was 1NT a simple raise will show a maximum 8 or 9 HCP with an 8-card fit.

Game raises promise at least 13 HCP.

REBID NO TRUMPS

    1NT = 6-9 HCP;   2NT = 10-12 HCP;   3NT = 13-15 HCP;

After THREE suits have been mentioned, No Trumps should only be called holding a 'stop' in the unbid suit.

REBID YOUR OWN SUIT (unsupported by partner)

A non-jump rebid of your suit will only be 5 cards in an emergency.

A JUMP rebid in your suit GUARANTEES at least 6.

2 level = 6-9 HCP; 3 level = 10-12 HCP; Game = 13-15 HCP

REBID YOUR OWN SUIT (supported by partner)

PASS	= 25 HCP are not possible (unless very shapely).
INVITE	= 25 HCP are possible opposite a maximum.
GAME	= 25 HCP are guaranteed or you are very shapely.

INTRODUCE A THIRD SUIT

A new suit BELOW two of the suit you first responded in is NON-FORCING with at least a 5-4 distribution.

A new suit ABOVE two of the suit you first responded in is FORCING for at least one round suggesting a 5-4 distribution and 11+ HCP.

A NEW SUIT INTRODUCED AT THE 3-LEVEL IS GAME-FORCING.

INTRODUCE THE FOURTH SUIT

Conventional. WATCH THIS SPACE! In the meantime avoid bidding the 4th suit naturally. Prefer to introduce No Trumps.

HOT TIP SUMMARY TABLE
FOR RESPONDING TO A REVERSE

THE REVERSE IS FORCING TO GAME when opener has bid a 3rd suit above the barrier;

(A) with 16+ HCP after any two-level response.

(B) with 19 HCP if forced to jump the bidding in order to get over the barrier after a one-level response.

RESPONSES
All bids are now forcing to at least game as 25 HCP are guaranteed.

'Fast arrival' to a game contract is a sign of weakness with no slam interest opposite a minimum reverse.

Other bids either harbour slam ambitions or express some uncertainty about the final contract.

THE REVERSE IS FORCING FOR ONE ROUND when opener has bid a 3rd suit above the barrier;

(C) with 16-19 HCP after a one-level response without jumping the bidding.

RESPONSES
Remember you MUST respond even with only 6 HCP.

With 6 or 7 HCP make a noise at the lowest available level. This bid can be passed. It may be a preference bid, a rebid of your own suit or a No Trump call.

With 8+ HCP you must either bid game directly – if you know which one to bid – or make a bid that partner cannot pass below game, like a jump bid or a bid of the 4th suit.

HANDY HINTS

To introduce a new suit at the three level in a constructive auction – by opener or responder – indicates that the partnership has enough points to bid a game. Therefore, the bidding must not stop until game has been reached.

Having initially shown an unlimited hand and flown the nest by changing the suit consider bringing your hand to roost with a descriptive, limited rebid at your next turn.

POINTS TO PONDER

If partner has shown a 5-4 shape only 4 cards remain a mystery.

Try and draw inferences from the way the auction has progressed.

The structure of reverse bidding (crossing the barrier) is designed to protect the partnership from getting too high on minimal values.

SMALL, MEDIUM & LARGE should form an integral part of your bidding strategy whether you are opener or responder.

(B) INTRODUCE THE FOURTH SUIT

♠ KQJ65
♡ 53
♢ 765
♣ AK4

At the end of the last quiz I posed this problem: After the auction starts 1♡ - 1♠ - 2♣ - ? what is your rebid?

With clearly enough points to bid a game (13 HCP) how should you proceed? You cannot make a jump rebid of 3♠ as this would show 10-12 HCP and a 6-card suit. You cannot raise either hearts or clubs without a known 8-card fit. It would be folly to suggest No Trumps with such a poor holding in diamonds (the unbid suit) and you are too strong to pass. HELP!

When all else fails and there doesn't appear to be a bid to describe your hand, bridge has a fairy godmother called FOURTH-SUIT FORCING. She can rescue you at awkward moments and generally save you from despair. But, like all women, she must be treated with respect. She will not forgive those who misuse her!

If you held length in the unbid suit ie. the FOURTH SUIT you would surely be considering a No Trump contract. After all, if partner has two suits and you have the other two suits the chances of having an 8-card fit in the unmentioned suit are slim. So what's the point of bidding it? You are about to find out!

"FOURTH-SUIT FORCING" is exactly what it says! i.e. when you have bid three suits naturally in a constructive auction the fourth suit is now bid as an ARTIFICIAL one-round force.

It is used when you want to keep the bidding open, but cannot accurately describe your hand.

IT SAYS NOTHING ABOUT YOUR HOLDING IN THE FOURTH SUIT!

The message to partner is:

"PLEASE DESCRIBE YOUR HAND FURTHER"

HOT TIP

HEALTH WARNING: Do not use Fourth-Suit Forcing on hands where you already have a perfectly good bid available.

RULES FOR FOURTH-SUIT FORCING

1. Fourth-Suit Forcing promises at least 11 HCP and is UNLIMITED.

2. When introduced at the one or two level it is only forcing for one round.

    Therefore the following responses may be passed:

    All responses by opener up to and including 2NT.
    1♡ - 1♠ - 2♣ - 2◊ - 2NT

    Simple (non-jump) preference to responder's suit.
    1♡ - 1♠ - 2♣ - 2◊ - 2♠

    Rebid of opener's first suit.
    1♡ - 1♠ - 2♣ - 2◊ - 2♡

    Any continuation of these auctions by responder is now game-forcing.

3. All other responses by opener are forcing to game:

    Jump preference to responder's suit.
    1♡ - 1♠ - 2♣ - 2◊ - 3♠

    Jump rebid in own suit.
    1♡ - 1♠ - 2♣ - 2◊ - 3♡

    Shape-showing 5/5 hands.
    1♡ - 1♠ - 2♣ - 2◊ - 3♣

4. When Fourth-Suit Forcing is introduced at the three level it is game-forcing.

    1♠ - 2♣ - 2♡ - 3◊
    1♡ - 1♠ - 2◊ - 3♣

5. When responding to Fourth-Suit Forcing you are required to clarify your hand pattern and strength. In all cases bid the maximum of your hand. Priority is given to:

    (a)   Showing a stop in the fourth suit for No Trumps.
           1♡ - 1♠ - 2◊ - 3♣ - 3NT

    (b)   Showing delayed support for partner's suit.
           1♡ - 2♣ - 2◊ - 2♠ - 3♣

    (c)   Indicating any extra shape not yet shown.
           1♣ - 1♡ - 1♠ - 2◊ - 2♠

RULE

Fourth-Suit Forcing used after a reverse creates a game force. The minimum number of points you thus require will correspond to the minimum number of points shown by partner's reverse.

HOT TIP

If you have bid three suits and you hold four cards in the fourth suit it is probably right to bid No Trumps at the appropriate level.

EXAMPLE AUCTION: 1♡ - 2♣ - 2◇ - ? (→ 15 HCP)   small

♠ 876	♠ KJ7	♠ 864	♠ 42	♠ AK2
♡ 65	♡ A2	♡ Q2	♡ A7	♡ 95
◇ AQJ	◇ J76	◇ KQJ5	◇ KQ54	◇ QJ2
♣ KQJ65	♣ AJ987	♣ QJ87	♣ AJ765	♣ Q8543

2♠	3NT	3◇	2♠	2NT
FSF			FSF	

EXAMPLE AUCTION: 1♠ - 2◇ - 2♡ - ? (→ 15 HCP)   small

♠ K87	♠ Q3	♠ J	♠ 43	♠ J5
♡ Q32	♡ KQJ	♡ J7	♡ Q6	♡ K5
◇ A8765	◇ KJ432	◇ KQJ765	◇ KQ973	◇ AKQJ54
♣ Q6	♣ J73	♣ K432	♣ AKJ5	♣ 432

3♠	3♣	3◇	3NT	3♣
	FSF			FSF

EXAMPLE AUCTION: 1◇ - 1♠ - 2♣ - ? (→ 18 HCP) small or medium

♠ K7654	♠ AQJ765	♠ AKQ6	♠ KQ87	♠ J6543
♡ J65	♡ 63	♡ 654	♡ AQ2	♡ A2
◇ 987	◇ K87	◇ Q6	◇ 876	◇ 97
♣ Q2	♣ J4	♣ QJ65	♣ 862	♣ KQJ5

2◇	3♠	2♡	2NT	3♣
		FSF		

EXAMPLE AUCTION: 1♣ - 1♠ - 2◊ - ? (16-19 HCP) medium or large
(Note: Partner 'REVERSED' through the barrier)

♠ KQJ543	♠ J765	♠ 97432	♠ AK764	♠ QJ765
♡ 32	♡ 654	♡ AQJ	♡ 872	♡ KQJ5
◊ 765	◊ AJ5	◊ 432	◊ Q32	◊ 82
♣ 65	♣ 654	♣ 64	♣ J6	♣ 62
2♠	3♣	2NT	2♡	3NT
			FSF	

NOW TRY BEING THE OPENER – AND RESPOND TO FOURTH-SUIT FORCING!

EXAMPLE AUCTION: 1◊ - 1♠ - 2♣ - 2♡ - ? (→ 18 HCP) small or medium

♠ 3	♠ 3	♠ KQ6	♠ KQ6	♠ 3
♡ KQ6	♡ KQ6	♡ 3	♡ 3	♡ K5
◊ AJ654	◊ AJ654	◊ AJ654	◊ AJ654	◊ A8654
♣ Q432	♣ A432	♣ Q432	♣ A432	♣ KQJ43
2NT	3NT	2♠	3♠	3♣

EXAMPLE AUCTION: 1♡ - 1♠ - 2♣ - 2◊ - ? (→ 18 HCP) small or medium

♠ 6	♠ 2	♠ Q43	♠ 5	♠ J7
♡ KQJ5	♡ KQJ876	♡ J6543	♡ AKJ43	♡ Q7654
◊ QJ32	◊ A3	◊ 7	◊ 963	◊ KQ
♣ KQ76	♣ AJ65	♣ AKQ2	♣ KJ76	♣ A432
3NT	3♡	2♠	2♡	2NT

EXAMPLE AUCTION: 1♠ - 2♣ - 2◊ - 2♡ - ? (→ 15 HCP)   small

♠ KQJ43	♠ AQJ76	♠ AK765	♠ QJ8765	♠ KJ543
♡ 6	♡ KJ5	♡ 54	♡ A2	♡ AQ2
◊ KJ32	◊ J876	◊ KQ32	◊ AQJ5	◊ AJ54
♣ K76	♣ 2	♣ 42	♣ 5	♣ 3
3♣	2NT	2♠	3♠	3NT

EXAMPLE AUCTION: 1♠ - 2◊ - 2♡ - 3♣ - ? (→ 15 HCP)   small

♠ AQ862	♠ K8765	♠ KJ652	♠ KQJ76	♠ AJ8762
♡ KQJ7	♡ AKQJ6	♡ J765	♡ AQ32	♡ KQ32
◊ 432	◊ 2	◊ 54	◊ 7	◊ J7
♣ 2	♣ J6	♣ AK	♣ J82	♣ 2
3◊	3♡	3NT	3♠	3♠

EXAMPLE AUCTION: 1♣ - 1♠ - 2◊ - 2♡ - ? (16-19HCP) medium or large
(Note: You 'REVERSED' through the barrier)

♠ 6	♠ AQ2	♠ A7	♠ J5	♠ 5
♡ KQ2	♡ 5	♡ J5	♡ AJ	♡ A
◊ KJ87	◊ KQJ7	◊ AK87	◊ KQ76	◊ KQJ76
♣ AKJ65	♣ AK765	♣ KJ876	♣ AJ876	♣ AK8765
3NT	3♠	2♠	2NT	3◊

If you have survived reading this book this far, it won't have escaped your notice that the game is full of rules. Hands-on experience will reveal the numerous exceptions to these rules with a few ifs and buts thrown in for good measure. Don't let this put you off! It is the idiosyncrasies of bridge that keep the game alive and make it so exciting!

Chapter Seven

OPENING WITH STRONG HANDS

(A) OPENING 2NT

Balanced hands with more than 19 HCP should be opened at the two level. This will give partner a clear message that game might be possible even when they have been dealt less than 6 HCP.

> **RULE**
>
> A 2NT opening bid is a limit bid showing a balanced hand with precisely 20-22 HCP and, therefore, it is non-forcing.

While it is preferable to hold a balanced hand to open 2NT, the lack of space involved in starting the bidding at this level allows for some flexibility within the definition. This means that some semi-balanced 5-4-2-2 hands in the 20-22 point zone should also be opened 2NT.

It is not unheard of to also include 4-4-4-1 hands in this point range which contain a singleton Ace or King. However, these instances are significantly infrequent and this inelegant shape might be better served with an opening bid at the one level in any case. Again the need to hold honour cards in every suit is not a prerequisite to this opening bid.

Responses to 2NT are reasonably straight forward. Unlike responding to 1NT, though, there is no weak takeout available so it is all or nothing as far as being in game is concerned. The only way to stop in a partscore is to PASS! General principles associated with responding to 1NT still apply. So, "No shortage, no Stayman" is still the order of the day, and you should prefer playing in 3NT with a five or six-card minor suit as against a minor suit game unless you are particularly distributional.

While 4 HCP is the normal minimum for a response, trump suit games can often manage on less than the usual 25 HCP required when very shapely. A fit of some description is already guaranteed (partner has at least a doubleton) so remember to add points for extra shape.

Classic 2NT openers will look like these:

♠ AK43	♠ K65	♠ KJ765	♠ AQ6	♠ QJ7
♡ KQ2	♡ AQJ52	♡ K3	♡ 54	♡ AKQ4
◇ J76	◇ KQ6	◇ AQJ6	◇ AKJ	◇ KJ
♣ AK7	♣ AJ	♣ AK	♣ AK854	♣ KQJ3
20 HCP	20 HCP	21 HCP	21 HCP	22 HCP

RESPONDING TO A 2NT OPENER

PASS = 0-3 HCP (unless very distributional).

3♣ = STAYMAN convention. Asking for 4-card majors. *(May have 5-4 in both majors for this bid.)* 3◇ by opener denies a major suit. Responder either supports opener's major or rebids 3NT. Responder will only bid a major suit at the three level with a 5-card suit.

3◇ = 5+ diamonds. Unsure about 3NT. Will usually have either 6 diamonds or at least 5-4 in both minors.

3♡/♠ = 5-card suit. Looking for 3 or 4-card support. Opener raises the major with 3+ support or rebids 3NT with a doubleton.

3NT = 4-10 HCP. To play. A sign-off bid. No interest in a major-suit game or a slam.

4♣ = The GERBER convention. To be used on slam hands to ask for Aces. See Chapter Ten.

4◇ = 6+ diamonds. Slam ambitions. 10+ HCP or extremely distributional.

4♡/♠ = At least a 6-card suit with game values but no interest in a slam. To play. A sign-off bid.

4NT = Quantitative. 11-12 HCP balanced. Asks opener to pass with 20 or 21 HCP. Asks opener to bid 6NT with 22 HCP.

5NT = Quantitative. 15-16 HCP balanced. Asks opener to bid 6NT with 20 or 21 HCP. Asks opener to bid 7NT with 22 HCP.

6NT = 13-14 HCP. Balanced. A sign-off bid.

7NT = 17-20 HCP. Balanced. A sign-off bid.

Oh! Did I say the responses were straightforward? Well, they will be when you have understood some of the principles of slam bidding.

Suffice to say for now that to make a Small Slam (12 tricks) in No Trumps when both hands are balanced you will usually require a minimum of 33 HCP. Grand Slams (13 tricks) are generally successful with a combined total of 37 HCP.

Chapter Ten dedicates itself to slam bidding and you will understand Chapters Seven and Nine more fully when this topic is conquered.

EXAMPLE HANDS: Select your response to partner's 2NT opening.

♠ 7654	♠ Q874	♠ QJ7654	♠ K3	♠ J76
♡ 973	♡ AJ752	♡ K76	♡ A7	♡ Q7
♢ 432	♢ 2	♢ J6	♢ J9865	♢ AQ432
♣ Q75	♣ 654	♣ J5	♣ J952	♣ Q54
2 HCP	7 HCP	8 HCP	9 HCP	11 HCP
Pass	3♣	4♠	3NT	4NT

EXAMPLE HANDS: Select your response to partner's 2NT opening.

♠ K98765	♠ KQ764	♠ A53	♠ Q2	♠ KQ3
♡ 43	♡ 73	♡ Q86542	♡ AK4	♡ AJ7
♢ 52	♢ J76	♢ QJ2	♢ Q654	♢ KJ43
♣ 872	♣ Q63	♣ 5	♣ J642	♣ J42
3 HCP	8 HCP	9 HCP	12 HCP	15 HCP
4♠	3♠	4♡	4NT	5NT

EXAMPLE HANDS: Select your response to partner's 2NT opening.

♠ Q872	♠ 32	♠ 2	♠ 6	♠ AKJ6
♡ Q532	♡ AQJ73	♡ 953	♡ Q53	♡ J64
♢ 32	♢ 86	♢ AQJ654	♢ AQJ654	♢ K74
♣ 872	♣ 6532	♣ 876	♣ K76	♣ Q32
4 HCP	7 HCP	7 HCP	12 HCP	14 HCP
3♣	3♡	3NT	4♢	6NT

(B) OPENING 2♣

The opening bid of 2♣ is the strongest opening bid you can make in the Acol system.

It is completely artificial and says absolutely nothing about clubs. (Just like the Stayman 2♣ convention).

RULE

It is used to open the bidding with hands that have either 23+ HCP or a powerful distribution with approximately 5 "QUICK TRICKS" and enough playing strength to attempt game even opposite NOTHING!

Because 2♣ is artificial it is 100% FORCING! Anyone found passing this bid will be severely punished!

The partner of the 2♣ opener has an immediate priority to reveal something about their point range, regardless of their hand pattern. Responder's hand falls into one of two categories. A NEGATIVE or a POSITIVE.

2◊   =   A NEGATIVE and 0-6 HCP. This bid is also
                                artificial and says nothing about diamonds.
                                This is clearly a FORCING manoeuvre too!

ANYTHING ELSE   =   A POSITIVE and 7+ HCP.

A negative response does not mean you have insufficient strength for a game or even a slam. It is purely a courtesy bid to give partner some indication of your side's combined strength. It can be concealing all sorts of weird and wonderful distributions – just like the 2♣ opening bid does. But, for the time being, it keeps the bidding nice and low for exploratory purposes.

If the 2♣ opener has a balanced hand its natural rebid will be some number of No Trumps. Facing a 'blizzard' (a hand with no points) game will be a tall order.

RULE

For this reason the sequence 2♣ - 2◊ - 2NT can be passed. In fact this is the ONLY auction that can be passed below game after a 2♣ opener.

But don't forget that just 2 measly HCP will aggregate 25 HCP and can offer serious game prospects.

By contrast, any positive response is likely to propel the partnership into the slam zone with a known minimum of 30 HCP. Having announced a powerhouse, making the correct rebid is clearly imperative. It is easy to get lost in an auction where you have begun by introducing artificial bids.

It is worth reiterating at this point that the sequence 2♣ - 2◇ - 2NT, which, incidentally, indicates that the opener has 23 or 24 HCP and a balanced hand, MAY be passed.

ANY OTHER SEQUENCE IS 100% FORCING TO AT LEAST GAME.

This simple rule may not appear to be too difficult to remember but you would be surprised how many bridge players are tempted to bow out below game after a 2♣ opener when they think that they have a bad hand. But remember that opposite a 2◇ negative any rebid other than 2NT will automatically show that the opener has either a balanced hand with 25+ HCP or ANY SHAPE that is willing to go to game opposite nothing. CONVINCED? You should be!

No doubt you are wondering about those "QUICK TRICKS" I mentioned earlier. Well, it's basically what is says. They are tricks that can be taken quickly!

$$A = 1 \qquad AK = 2 \qquad AQ = 1\frac{1}{2} \qquad KQ = 1 \qquad Kx = \frac{1}{2}$$

The primary reason for putting this factor into the equation will become more meaningful when you encounter interference from the opposition. Yes, opponents can do damage to your auction even when you have attempted to frighten them off with your incredible strength. More about that in Chapter Twelve.

Here are some typical 2♣ openers:

♠ AKQJ765	♠ AK5	♠ K2	♠ AQJ3	♠ AQ6
♡ A	♡ KQJ52	♡ K3	♡ KJ7	♡ A4
◇ AK2	◇ KQ5	◇ AKQJ4	◇ A43	◇ AK
♣ 43	♣ AJ	♣ AK76	♣ AKQ	♣ AKJ876
21 HCP	23 HCP	23 HCP	24 HCP	25 HCP

RESPONSES TO 2♣

2◊	=	0-6 HCP. NEGATIVE. ANY SHAPE.
2♡/♠	=	7+ HCP. Good quality 5+ suit.
2NT	=	7-9 HCP. Balanced.
3♣/◊	=	7+ HCP. Good quality 5+ suit.
3♡/♠	=	No loser 6+ suit. 10+ HCP.
3NT	=	10-12 HCP. Balanced.
4♣/◊	=	No loser 6+ suit. 10+ HCP.

RULE

Do not make a positive response by bidding a 4-card suit. You can bid a 4-card suit, if necessary, on the next round – if supporting partner or rebidding No Trumps are not attractive options.

RULE

'Good quality' is generally defined as having two of the top three honours. Distributional factors and common sense do allow some flexibility into this rule, however.

EXAMPLE HANDS: Select the correct response to partner's 2♣ opening bid:

♠ 543	♠ 93	♠ J3	♠ Q87	♠ AK987
♡ 9752	♡ AQ765	♡ AQ765	♡ K76	♡ 3
◊ 5	◊ 974	◊ 974	◊ 876	◊ K876
♣ 98542	♣ 942	♣ 942	♣ QJ83	♣ Q32
0 HCP	6 HCP	7 HCP	8 HCP	12 HCP
2◊	2◊	2♡	2NT	2♠

EXAMPLE HANDS: Select the correct response to partner's 2♣ opening bid:

♠ Q84	♠ J8765	♠ K2	♠ AKQJ86	♠ QJ5
♡ 32	♡ Q2	♡ 753	♡ 984	♡ QJ87
◇ KQJ876	◇ Q54	◇ 87	◇ 74	◇ K652
♣ 32	♣ KJ8	♣ AQJ765	♣ 98	♣ K7
8 HCP	9 HCP	10 HCP	10 HCP	12 HCP
3◇	2NT	3♣	3♠	3NT

REBIDS BY OPENER AFTER THE AUCTION HAS STARTED
2♣ - 2◇ - ?

2♡/♠	=	At least a 5-card suit.	GAME FORCING.
2NT	=	23 or 24 HCP. Balanced.	NON-FORCING.
3♣/◇	=	At least a 5-card suit.	GAME FORCING.
3♡/♠	=	No loser 6+ suit.	GAME FORCING.
3NT	=	25-28 HCP. Balanced.	GAME FORCING.
4♣/◇	=	No loser 6+ suit.	GAME FORCING.

HOT TIP

Following the sequence 2♣ - 2◇ - 2NT responder should reply as if partner had opened the bidding with 2NT. BUT, remember to modify the point count responses by 2 HCP.

EXAMPLE HANDS: Make your rebid after the auction has started 2♣ - 2◇ - ?

♠ KJ864	♠ AKQJ	♠ K7	♠ AQJ75	♠ AKQ
♡ AQJ	♡ 4	♡ AKJ876	♡ AKJ6	♡ AK84
◇ KQ	◇ KQJ963	◇ AKQ2	◇ AK	◇ KJ
♣ AK4	♣ AK	♣ A	♣ K4	♣ KQJ5
23 HCP	23 HCP	24 HCP	25 HCP	26 HCP
2NT	3◇	2♡	2♠	3NT

EXAMPLE HANDS: Make your rebid after the auction has started 2♣ - 2◊ - ?

♠ AQ	♠ -	♠ AQ6	♠ AKQ4	♠ AKQJ765
♡ K3	♡ AKQ76	♡ A4	♡ KQ4	♡ A
◊ AQJ2	◊ AKQ54	◊ AK	◊ AKJ7	◊ AK2
♣ AK864	♣ AK3	♣ AKJ876	♣ QJ	♣ 43
23 HCP	25 HCP	25 HCP	25 HCP	21 HCP
2NT	2♡	3♣	3NT	3♠

REBIDS BY OPENER AFTER A POSITIVE RESPONSE

After a positive response rebids by opener in a new suit are natural with at least five cards. With a known combined minimum of 30 HCP between the two hands there is plenty of scope for a small or grand slam to be bid and made. If you can find the right trump fit nature usually takes its course and before you know it you'll be at the dizzy heights of the six or seven level.

> ### HOT TIP
>
> If either hand has shown a 5-card suit don't forget to support them holding three or more yourself.

At this point I could frighten you even more with a lot more scientific and technical sequences in continuation. However, fortunately, or unfortunately as the case may be, the frequency of these strong opening bids does not warrant any further investigation at this stage of your development.

Once again, I confess that your slam bidding experience has, so far in this book, been negligible. So, until the relevant chapters have been digested things may seem a teeny weeny bit bleak.

(C) OPENING 2◊ or 2♡ or 2♠

Occasionally you will pick up powerful one- or two-suited hands on which you might be able to make game opposite a hand with less than 6 HCP.

e.g.

♠ AQJ987
♡ AKQ5
◊ A2
♣ 4

It would be a tragedy to be left playing in One Spade when game is a doddle opposite hand (a), and hand (b) offers slam potential:

(a)		(b)	
	♠ K43		♠ 6
	♡ J76		♡ J987
	◊ 8765		◊ 9754
	♣ 987		♣ A652

If you risk opening hands like these at the one level, and partner holds less than 6 HCP, that is likely to become the final contract and your chance of a game or slam bonus has gone out of the window.

So, why not open Two Clubs? If you remember, a Two Club opening bid will always propel you into game unless your hand is balanced with 23 or 24 HCP.

What you need to do is to create an opportunity to investigate the chance of game without a firm commitment. In other words you need a get-out at the three level if partner can't come up with the goods.

An opening bid of 2◊, 2♡ or 2♠ caters for these types of hands which are not strong enough to be opened with a game-forcing Acol 2♣, but are clearly too powerful for the auction to be started at the one level.

Generally, hands which merit an opening bid of a suit at the two level will have somewhere between 20 and 22 HCP. However, this will not always be the case when you consider extra distributional features.

This next rule is regarded as the major factor in estimating your true strength.

RULE

If you are going to start the auction at the two level in a suit you need sufficient playing strength to generate at least 8 playing tricks.

TO CALCULATE PLAYING TRICKS COUNT:

A   = 1   K   = ½   AK   = 2   KQ = 1

AQJ = 2   KQJ = 2   AKQ = 3   AQ = 1½

and count every card AFTER the third card in that suit as a winner.
e.g.

AKQxxxx = 7 tricks   AQJxxxx = 6 tricks

AKxxxxx = 6 tricks   Axxxxx   = 4 tricks

KQJxxx   = 5 tricks   KJxxxx   = 3½ tricks

KQxxxx   = 4 tricks   AQxxxx = 4½ tricks

This is only a guide to help you count potential tricks. Adverse
distributions can obviously effect the outcome in real life!

RULE

Another important condition is that your hand should contain a
minimum of two quick tricks outside your nominated trump suit.

i.e.   ♠ AKQJ9876
                  ♡ 54
                  ◇ 8
                  ♣ 82

is not worthy of an Acol Two opener despite having the wherewithal to make
eight tricks in spades. But ...

                  ♠ AKQJ98
                  ♡ A5
                  ◇ A76
                  ♣ 82

is certainly adequate with its two defensive tricks – and only 18 HCP!

Here are some hands which qualify as an Acol Two opener:

♠ -	♠ 6	♠ KQJ987	♠ K65	♠ AKQ86
♡ AKQ543	♡ AK7	♡ AK	♡ AKJ765	♡ KQ987
◇ AKQ2	◇ AKJ9876	◇ KQJ	◇ AKQ	◇ A4
♣ 543	♣ A5	♣ 53	♣ 9	♣ A
18 HCP	19 HCP	19 HCP	20 HCP	22 HCP
2♡	2◇	2♠	2♡	2♠

Note that none of the examples includes hands with 8 or more playing tricks in clubs. This highlights a problem area which will surface every once in a while when this type of hand rears its head. Your judgement will dictate its fate. Choices available to you will include 1♣, 2NT or at a pinch 2♣ as opening bids.

RULE

Responder is not allowed to pass your Acol Two opening bid. It is FORCING FOR ONE ROUND.

RESPONSES TO AN ACOL TWO OPENING BID:

Once again, responder's priority is to give partner an indication of their point range.

2NT	=	A NEGATIVE and 0-7 HCP. It is completely artificial and has no relevance to the shape of the hand actually held.
ANYTHING ELSE	=	A POSITIVE and 8+ HCP*.

* Well, as usual there is an exception so here is the complete set of responses:

RESPONSES TO AN ACOL TWO OPENING BID

An Acol 2◇, 2♡, or 2♠ opening bid is FORCING FOR ONE ROUND.

1. Respond 2NT with 0-7 HCP to show a NEGATIVE. (see 6)

2. Any other response is a POSITIVE and 100% FORCING TO GAME.

3. A simple rebid of opener's suit after a negative response may be passed.

4. A change of suit by opener even after a negative response is FORCING FOR ONE ROUND.

5. A simple raise by responder shows 3+ support and 8+ HCP. It is unlimited and can be very strong.

6. A double raise by responder shows 6-7 HCP (i.e. top of the negative range) and 4+ trump support. *(This is the exception to Response 1)*

7. A response of 3NT shows a balanced hand with 8-10 HCP but denies three cards in partner's major suit.

EXAMPLE HANDS: Select your response after partner has opened 2♡ - ?

♠ K76	♠ 654	♠ 54	♠ KQJ98	♠ J72
♡ -	♡ J876	♡ K974	♡ 54	♡ K98
◇ 5432	◇ J63	◇ K974	◇ Q86	◇ J765
♣ 987654	♣ Q42	♣ 532	♣ 654	♣ K87
3 HCP	4 HCP	6 HCP	8 HCP	8 HCP
2NT	2NT	4♡	2♠	3♡

EXAMPLE HANDS: Select your response after partner has opened 2♠ - ?

♠ 2	♠ KJ76	♠ A76	♠ 75	♠ J6
♡ 9753	♡ 52	♡ KJ765	♡ QJ76	♡ AK876
◇ 8654	◇ Q76	◇ 975	◇ QJ62	◇ 7632
♣ 7532	♣ J876	♣ 75	♣ K75	♣ Q2
0 HCP	7 HCP	8 HCP	9 HCP	10 HCP
2NT	4♠	3♠	3NT	3♡

EXAMPLE HANDS: Select your response after partner has opened 2◊ - ?

♠ QJ7654	♠ KQJ43	♠ 4	♠ QJ6	♠ AK54
♡ K876	♡ K2	♡ AQ654	♡ AJ65	♡ 54
◊ -	◊ 54	◊ 43	◊ 32	◊ J876
♣ 654	♣ 6543	♣ K8642	♣ J976	♣ K42
6 HCP	9 HCP	9 HCP	9 HCP	11 HCP
2NT	2♠	2♡	3NT	3◊

HANDY HINTS

Before opening at the two level ask yourself if you might miss a game if you open the bidding at the one level.

While a lot of distributional hands qualify for an Acol 2♣ opener most strong two-suited hands are still best opened at the two level with a genuine suit. This makes subsequent bidding easier if the opponents intervene.

POINT TO PONDER

An Acol 2◊, 2♡ or 2♠ opening bid may be stronger than an Acol 2♣ opener, but in playing strength – not points.

Chapter Eight

PREEMPTIVE OPENING BIDS

With the serious business of opening the bidding with strength under your belt it's time to let your hair down!

Seemingly throwing caution to the wind you can actually open the bidding higher than the two level with hands that were even too weak to be opened at the one level! Double-Dutch? Let me explain.

The game of Bridge is all about scoring. Your immediate aim is to achieve a plus score. However, if you are outgunned in the points zone that is often an impossible target. Your task in those situations is to keep your losses to a minimum.

When you pick up a good hand you will want as much space as possible to explore for the right contract. Imagine your right-hand opponent opening the bidding at the three level and it's not too difficult to envisage the damage this might inflict to your side. Before you have had a chance to communicate with partner you may be forced to guess whether you should be ...

... bidding or not?

... playing the hand or defending?

While it is a perfectly legitimate ploy to make it difficult for the opponents to gauge their combined assets by preempting the auction there is no merit in bidding indiscriminately. Apart from the fact that the contract may actually belong to the 'preempting' side there are large penalties to be gleaned from those who dangerously overbid.

Cast an eye over the page on penalty scores at the front of this book and this aspect becomes clearer.

That said, there is a code of conduct for the requirements to open at a high level. You are not expected to be clairvoyant on every hand, but if you follow some simple guidelines it will help you stay out of trouble.

(A) AN OPENING BID OF A SUIT AT THE THREE LEVEL

RULE

A three-level preemptive opening bid shows a GOOD QUALITY 7-card suit and 6-10 HCP.

This well-defined manoeuvre is a limit bid. You will be accurately describing your hand pattern and strength within a narrow band of points. As previously mentioned, it is the partner of the limit-bidder who controls the subsequent auction for their side.

With such a weak hand you are obviously not expecting to make nine tricks unless partner holds some points. Apart from robbing the opposition of their bidding space your objective is to offer yourself as a sacrifice! You are tempting opponents to take what may be an inferior score to that of a game or slam they can make.

Here are some hands which qualify for a preempt;

♠ KQJ8765	♠ 43	♠ Q3	♠ A3	♠ AJ98732
♡ 76	♡ AQJ7654	♡ 6	♡ 32	♡ 75
◊ 752	◊ 73	◊ AQ98765	◊ 32	◊ K4
♣ 2	♣ 82	♣ 432	♣ KJ97654	♣ J3
6 HCP	7 HCP	8 HCP	8 HCP	9 HCP
3♠	3♡	3◊	3♣	3♠

These hands deliberately avoid any examples of 7-4 distributions where your second suit is a major. Of course, this does not mean you are not allowed to include such hands in your repertoire. Just be aware of the possible repercussions of having an undisclosed major-suit fit. Your valiant efforts in the preemptive zone are designed to restrict the opponent's options – not inconvenience partner!

Note also the concentration of values and intermediates in your long suit. With so few points required for this call your good quality suit must exude playing strength and will automatically preclude much defensive strength. This is the ultimate recipe for success!

HOT TIP

Vulnerability also plays a significant part in determining your fate. Suffice to say you should exercise more caution when vulnerable – especially if opponents are not. Similarly, you can be a little more adventurous when this aspect is reversed.

RESPONDING TO PARTNER'S THREE-LEVEL PREEMPT

Given that partner has a weak hand and the bid is limited it is certainly not forcing. You are only advised to respond when you have one of the following hand types:

a) 16+ HCP or

b) A weaker hand with at least a 3-card trump fit or

c) A weaker hand with substantial playing strength in its own right.

Except for a change of suit being forcing for one round and all game bids 'to play' there are no hard and fast rules. Your guiding light will often be just common sense.

EXAMPLE HANDS: Select a sensible response to partner's 3♣ opening bid:

♠ K6	♠ A654	♠ KQ9765	♠ AJ	♠ AQ2
♡ 3	♡ KQJ7	♡ AK	♡ QJ8	♡ QJ6
◊ A87654	◊ J876	◊ K87	◊ AKQ9876	◊ KQ32
♣ KJ54	♣ 5	♣ J5	♣ 7	♣ KJ6
II HCP	II HCP	16 HCP	17 HCP	18 HCP
5♣	Pass	3♠	3NT	3NT

EXAMPLE HANDS: Select a sensible response to partner's 3♡ opening bid:

♠ J876	♠ AKQJ876	♠ A54	♠ A543	♠ AKQJ
♡ 6	♡ 76	♡ A	♡ AQ6	♡ KQ3
◊ AQJ876	◊ 7	◊ A543	◊ A43	◊ A74
♣ Q2	♣ Q32	♣ A8743	♣ QJ7	♣ KQ6
10 HCP	12 HCP	16 HCP	17 HCP	24 HCP
Pass	4♠	4♡	3NT	4NT!
				(see page 121)

(B) AN OPENING BID OF 3NT

While we're on the subject of opening the bidding at the three level allow me to introduce you to the Gambling 3NT opener. This call describes a rare bird indeed. None the less its message would, otherwise, be impossible to convey accurately with any other choice of opening bid. Take a look.

Here are four typical 3NT opening bids:

♠ Q2	♠ J32	♠ 976	♠ J54
♡ 54	♡ 4	♡ 753	♡ J4
◇ 72	◇ AKQJ875	◇ AKQJ432	◇ J
♣ AKQJ654	♣ 32	♣ -	♣ AKQJ974
12 HCP	11 HCP	10 HCP	13 HCP

Promising a solid 7-card minor and at most a King outside, the scene is set. Another example of a non-forcing limit bid allows you to sit back and leave all the decision-making to your trusted partner!

Of course, you may still have a very important part to play so don't fall asleep.

RESPONDING TO PARTNER'S 3NT OPENER

a) Pass   =   Happy to 'gamble'. Will probably have a stopper or two in the majors and, hopefully, the other minor.

b) 4♣   =   This is a weak take-out to play in OPENER'S minor. Opener passes with clubs and bids 4◇ with diamonds.

c) 4NT   =   To play game or slam in OPENER'S minor. Spare a thought for partner who may not have a clue which minor suit you are holding! Convert to the five level *au naturel*.

d) Bid game =   To play.

EXAMPLE HANDS: Select a sensible response to partner's 3NT opening bid:

♠ QJ65	♠ AK3	♠ AKJ9876	♠ AQ32	♠ K32
♡ AJ95	♡ 6	♡ AQ	♡ KQ43	♡ AK65
◇ KQ32	◇ 8765	◇ 32	◇ AQ432	◇ 54
♣ 7	♣ KQJ43	♣ 32	♣ -	♣ AKQ2
13 HCP	13 HCP	14 HCP	17 HCP	19 HCP
Pass	5◇	4♠	5♣	6◇

(C) AN OPENING BID OF A SUIT AT THE FOUR LEVEL

... and so the saga goes on. A level higher shows a different style and strength of preempt, though it's still based on a long suit.

You might recall a hand from Chapter Seven on Acol Two openers where I said you were unsuitable for a Two Spade opening bid holding;

♠ AKQJ9876
♡ 54
◊ 8
♣ 82

Surprise surprise – it's a perfect hand for opening Four Spades! If partner produces a pathetic display of points you won't be making this contract – but the good news is that your opponents have been barraged out of an auction at a very high level with little hope of discovering their true potential until the smoke has cleared!

To sum up, you are taking an instinctive gamble that the four level is the limit of your side's strength. Even if you are wrong it should only be low risk in your heroic attempt to outwit the opposition.

Here are a modest collection of four-level preempts:

♠ KJ1098765	♠ AK98765	♠ 5
♡ A32	♡ -	♡ AKQJ876
◊ 5	◊ QJ76	◊ J987
♣ 4	♣ 76	♣ 2
8 HCP	10 HCP	11 HCP
4♠	4♠	4♡

♠ 3	♠ -	♠ -
♡ 43	♡ KQ987654	♡ KQJ9654
◊ 54	◊ Q87	◊ 8
♣ KQJ87654	♣ 73	♣ QJ876
6 HCP	7 HCP	9 HCP
4♣	4♡	4♡!

See how few prospective defensive tricks each hand possesses.

HANDY HINTS

Once you have preempted you have done your bit. Let partner make the next move.

Don't forget the bid 'PASS' still exists! You may be tempted to have fun with an off-centre preempt, but not all partners will laugh when everything backfires!

Chapter Nine

JUMP SHIFTS BY RESPONDER

Taking a break from frivolity there is some unfinished business we need to attend to left over from Chapter Three.

You now have a sound knowledge of how to respond to partner's suit opening bid with 0-15 HCP. What about those occasions when you are blessed with more?

When you know you have oodles of points between you, it is easy to reach game. You may not always be sure which game, but you've usually got time to investigate all options. Hands which offer slam opportunities need to be handled with far more caution. It is easy to miscalculate your destination despite your combined strength, and to miss the boat or get a minus score would be a great pity. You need to know exactly where you're heading and this means that careful handling is required when you are about to respond with 16+ HCP.

Much of the time a simple (i.e. non-jump) response is still the best way forward. There is often no substitute for awaiting partner's natural rebid and then taking control on the next round of the auction.

There are some situations, however, when it is partner who is best placed to take control of your powerhouse. To be precise, THREE situations.

If you hold one of the following three types of hands your initial response should be in the form of a JUMP SHIFT. That means you will jump the bidding and shift suit simultaneously!

e.g.   1♣ - 2♠   or 1♡ - 3◇   etc.

The message is simple but you MUST obey one of the following criteria.

HAND TYPE ONE
16+ HCP (unlimited) with a good quality suit of 6+ cards in a single-suited hand.

e.g.

	♠ KQJ987	or	♠ AQJ8765
	♡ A2		♡ 8
	◇ K3		◇ AQ2
	♣ A73		♣ K2

Bid 2♠ over an opening bid of 1♣/1◇/1♡ with the intention of rebidding your spade suit on the next round. An example auction might proceed;
1♡ - 2♠ - 3♣ - 3♠ ...

e.g.

♠ AK	or	♠ J6
♡ 5		♡ A7
◇ QJ2		◇ K5
♣ AK87654		♣ AKQJ654

Bid 3♣ over an opening bid of 1◇/1♡/1♠ with the intention of rebidding clubs on the next round; e.g. 1♠ - 3♣ - 3♠ - 4♣ ...

HAND TYPE TWO

16+ HCP (unlimited) with a good quality suit of 5+ cards and 4+ cards in PARTNER'S suit.

e.g.

♠ AQJ76	or	♠ AK752
♡ A543		♡ KJ65
◇ K8		◇ AQ3
♣ Q2		♣ 2

Bid 2♠ over an opening bid of 1♡ ONLY with the intention of supporting partner's hearts on the next round; e.g. 1♡ - 2♠ - 3◇ - 3♡ ...

e.g.

♠ AK84	or	♠ QJ64
♡ 6		♡ KJ
◇ KQJ54		◇ AKQJ6
♣ A32		♣ J6

Bid 3◇ over an opening bid of 1♠ ONLY with the intention of supporting partner's spades on the next round; e.g. 1♠ - 3◇ - 3♡ - 3♠ ...

HAND TYPE THREE

16-18 HCP (LIMITED) with a good quality 5-card suit and a BALANCED hand. (i.e. 5-3-3-2 specifically)

e.g.

♠ KJ4	or	♠ A2
♡ Q2		♡ A85
◇ AQJ72		◇ KQ986
♣ K53		♣ AJ2

Bid 2◊ over an opening bid of 1♣, or bid 3◊ over an opening bid of either 1♡ or 1♠ with the intention of rebidding No Trumps on the next round; e.g. 1♣ - 2◊ - 2♡ - 2NT ...

e.g.

♠ AKQ52	or	♠ KQJ65
♡ Q65		♡ AJ2
◊ K2		◊ KQJ
♣ A42		♣ J5

Bid 2♠ over an opening bid of 1♣/1◊/1♡ with the intention of rebidding No Trumps on the next round; e.g. 1◊ - 2♠ - 3♣ - 3NT ...

There is a strong possibility that you will be side-tracked holding hand type three whenever partner indicates a 5-card major and you have 3-card support. It's not an unhappy situation, but bear in mind that when you do raise this suit – quite correctly – partner will expect to see hand type two.

HOT TIP

As you may remember balanced hands require at least 33 HCP between the two hands to contemplate a small slam. The limited point range for hand type three helps the partnership to monitor this requirement reasonably accurately. Do not be tempted to step outside this boundary! You have been warned!

To summarise, your jump shift will ALWAYS guarantee;

(a) At least 16 HCP.

(b) A good quality suit of at least 5 cards – by the way, the definition of 'good quality' in this context expects the suit to be headed by at least the Ace or King plus one other honour.

(c) No second suit unless it is a fit for partner.

RULE

If your hand does not meet with these requirements – DO NOT MAKE A JUMP SHIFT! Start with a SIMPLE response.

EXAMPLE HANDS: How would you respond to partner's opening bid of 1♣?

♠ K43	♠ A3	♠ KQJ654	♠ KJ654	♠ AQ65
♡ AKJ74	♡ 76	♡ J3	♡ AKQ65	♡ K87
♢ A32	♢ AKQ65	♢ AQ3	♢ AJ	♢ A3
♣ J5	♣ A865	♣ KQ	♣ 3	♣ KQJ6
16 HCP	17 HCP	18 HCP	18 HCP	19 HCP
2♡	2♢	2♠	1♠	1♠

EXAMPLE HANDS: How would you respond to partner's opening bid of 1♡?

♠ AK874	♠ Q8754	♠ 4	♠ AKJ63	♠ AQ
♡ KQ32	♡ AJ7	♡ AQ2	♡ J85	♡ QJ6
♢ 7	♢ A43	♢ AQJ854	♢ KQ2	♢ K54
♣ A98	♣ KQ	♣ AJ7	♣ AJ	♣ AKJ76
16 HCP	16 HCP	18 HCP	19 HCP	20 HCP
2♣	1♠	3♢	1♠	2♣

If you are still puzzled perhaps I can elucidate further.

QUESTION
Why don't we make a jump shift response on all hands with 16+ HCP?

ANSWER
Because a jump shift is space consuming, using up a whole level of bidding that can often be put to better use.

Any doubts about the best strain plus any degree of uncertainty regarding your total assets means you need as much room as possible to explore.

Also, opener's rebid will often be distorted following a jump shift. For a start, reversing 'barriers' no longer exist in the same way because it is not economical and, anyway, this information is not particularly useful anymore.

Secondly, if a jump shift shows at least a 5-card suit priority now goes to supporting this suit with just three cards. This would certainly not have been a natural rebid previously.

QUESTION
Why bother to jump shift at all then?

ANSWER
Because certain hand patterns – the three hand types specified – are awkward to describe accurately on the second round of the auction.

EXAMPLE HANDS: Make your rebid as opener: 1◊ - 2♡ - ?

♠ 65	♠ AJ76	♠ 3	♠ AQ6	♠ AQ4
♡ KJ76	♡ 32	♡ K74	♡ 6	♡ J8
◊ AQ432	◊ K8765	◊ AK872	◊ KQJ853	◊ Q8765
♣ Q2	♣ A2	♣ QJ63	♣ Q43	♣ KQJ
12 HCP	12 HCP	13 HCP	14 HCP	15 HCP
4♡	2♠	3♡	3◊	2NT

EXAMPLE HANDS: Make your rebid as opener: 1♡ - 3♣ - ?

♠ AK76	♠ Q87	♠ KQJ	♠ AK2	♠ KJ6
♡ AJ876	♡ KQ874	♡ 96543	♡ KJ753	♡ AKQ752
◊ 83	◊ KQJ5	◊ KQ3	◊ 4	◊ Q74
♣ 76	♣ 2	♣ A6	♣ KJ76	♣ Q
12 HCP	13 HCP	15 HCP	15 HCP	17 HCP
3♡	3◊	3NT	4♣	3♡

HOT TIP

Use of the jump shift implies you will be playing in either:

THE SUIT OPENED or
THE RESPONDER'S SUIT or
NO TRUMPS.

Now doesn't that make it sound easy?!

Way back on page 41, coping with as many as 15 HCP and 4-card support for partner's opening bid was your biggest headache. Should you be lucky enough to pick up 16 or more HCP, plus a fit, the chapter you have just read should help you decide how to respond. Remember the concept of jump-shifting and you will appreciate that without the necessary criteria you will simply have to make do with a temporising change of suit at the minimum level.

e.g.   1♠ - 2♣ holding

> ♠ A432
> ♡ Q98
> ◊ K2
> ♣ AQJ3

or   1♡ - 1♠ holding

> ♠ J987
> ♡ KQ42
> ◊ KQ3
> ♣ AJ

HANDY HINTS

If a jump shift promises at least 16 HCP in response to an opening bid you will NEVER stay out of game. Ergo, the auction is 100% forcing to game.

Remember that a simple change of suit is forcing.

Chapter Ten

SLAM BIDDING

If you always bid slams which make and avoid bidding the ones that can't you should be playing bridge for your country! Precision in the slam zone is as realistic as peace throughout the world! It's a dream.

If you never bid a slam in your life it will not be a tragedy. Boring, yes! It might even be winning bridge – long term – but you really would be missing out on a very exciting area of the game.

The challenge in bidding and making a slam has its own reward. Let's just say there is a feel-good factor involved as well as a slam bonus!

Having whetted your appetite I hope you won't be disappointed. I can give you some solid rules to follow. I can show you the ropes. But, at the end of the day experience is your only true guiding light.

You will need 13 tricks to make a grand slam and 12 tricks to make a small slam. A source of tricks and plenty of points are two of the main ingredients for a successful recipe. So, presuming the defence cannot take the first two tricks you must be in with a shout!

If you have decided that you have the combined strength to attempt a slam you should first check up on how many Aces and Kings your side holds before launching. This will save you the embarrassment of going down in your contract before you've even gained the lead!

Enter ...

(A) THE BLACKWOOD CONVENTION

Named after its inventor, Easley Blackwood, this is the simplest and most commonly used Ace-asking convention. While it is not sophisticated it is easy to remember.

Once you have agreed a trump suit or at least know in which trump suit you intend to play bid 4NT to ask for Aces.

RESPONSES TO 4NT

5♣	=	0 or 4 Aces
5♢	=	I Ace
5♡	=	2 Aces
5♠	=	3 Aces

Following the response to 4NT a bid of 5NT asks for Kings.

RESPONSES TO 5NT

6♣	=	0 Kings
6♢	=	1 King
6♡	=	2 Kings
6♠	=	3 Kings
6NT	=	4 Kings

Unfortunately slam bidding isn't just about using the Blackwood convention. It is all about being able to translate information received about the brute strength of your two hands into slam potential.

QUESTION
Which one of the partnership should use Blackwood?

ANSWER
You are both on the same ship and, as in real life, there should only be one captain! The controller will either be the person who holds the best hand or, more commonly, the partner of the limit bidder. Whatever else you do, please don't fight for the privilege of captaincy or you will both drown ...

Before looking at some slam sequences here are some guidelines to follow before considering the use of Blackwood.

1.   Blackwood is usually unsuitable for hands containing a void.

2.   You should never ask for Kings when there is an Ace missing. This is because a bid of 5NT guarantees all the Aces and partner is entitled to bid a grand slam directly over 5NT with extra values.

EXAMPLE 1

WEST	EAST
♠ AK987	♠ Q654
♡ KQJ53	♡ A42
◇ A6	◇ K98
♣ 2	♣ Q65

1♠	3♠
4NT	5◇
6♠	

With only 28 HCP between the two hands a small slam can be made. What are the most significant features for West to appreciate in determining his hand's slam potential? A good trump holding, a good quality 5-card side suit plus no wasted honour cards in the two short suits all combine to maximum effect. It is only when the dummy goes down that West can also see how well the two hands fit together. In 6♠ most of East's honour cards are useful, but a 6NT contract would not have a happy ending!

EXAMPLE 2

WEST	EAST
♠ A432	♠ KQJ98
♡ K2	♡ A3
◇ AJ	◇ K32
♣ A5432	♣ KQJ

1♣	1♠
3♠	4NT
5♠	5NT
6◇	7NT

East has slam ambitions as soon as West opens the bidding. Having located the fit East only needs to use Blackwood to establish the level. Opposite three Aces and a King a 7NT contract can be guaranteed by counting 5 spade tricks, 2 hearts, 2 diamonds and 4 clubs – even before the dummy goes down! That's the degree of certainty we would always like to achieve when bidding a grand slam!

EXAMPLE 3

WEST	EAST
♠ J	♠ KQ
♡ K43	♡ A82
◊ AK10876	◊ QJ9
♣ J32	♣ AK654

1◊	2♣
2◊	4NT
5◊	6◊

East is happy to drive to a slam even opposite a minimum opening bid. Missing an Ace the partnership has to settle for the six level. 6NT may look attractive but, despite having 30 HCP to play with and two long suits to develop, prospects are not as good as in 6◊. Best advice is to aim for the safest slam rather than gamble for a higher point score.

EXAMPLE 4

WEST	EAST
♠ AJ	♠ 865
♡ AQ7654	♡ KJ83
◊ KQJ8	◊ 97
♣ 2	♣ AKQ6

1♡	4♡
4NT	5◊
6♡	

An excellent heart slam is reached once West can be sure there are not two Aces missing. See the danger of playing in a No Trump contract on a spade lead.

QUESTION

What happens if the response to Blackwood shows there are two Aces missing and you have gone past five of the agreed trump suit?

ANSWER

This will only happen to you when you have agreed clubs as trumps. It's as well to anticipate this possibility before you use Blackwood, but there is a way to try and salvage the situation. Rather than accept defeat and bid a slam knowing the opponents can cash two Aces you might have the resources to make eleven tricks in No Trumps.

As a bid of 5NT asks for Kings you need to do something strange that will alert partner of the impending disaster. Bid a suit at the five level that has not been bid naturally by either of you in the auction to date. This is an SOS for partner to bid 5NT, which you will pass. Failing that a large G and T for partner will probably not go amiss!

A source of tricks and somewhere in the 30 HCP zone were clearly instrumental in bringing home the example slam hands.

What else did they have in common?

A near solid trump fit was also the key to success. Suit slams will obviously be more successful when you have at least nine trumps between you or at worst eight good ones.

The source of tricks you required came in the form of a second suit which always suggests an unbalanced hand.

Singletons and voids too exude tremendous power against the opponents' defence mechanism. Imagine their disappointment in Example 1 when only one trick can be taken holding both the Ace and King of clubs. Frustration too for the opposition in Example 3 when a losing club and the Ace of Spades would scupper 6NT, but not Six Diamonds where the club loser can be discarded on a spade and the club suit can be established by way of a ruff for a heart discard. Not to mention Example 4 where a spade lead would generate two tricks for the defence only to see one of them disappear on a winning club. The benefits of playing in a trump suit are all too apparent. You can trump your losers!

The conclusion one can thus draw is that a suit slam can be successful even when the partnership holds relatively few HCP providing the losers can be CONTROLLED!

ONE LAST QUESTION

Is it remotely possible that the opponents will intervene directly over 4NT before the response can be given? If so, how does one reply?

ONE LAST ANSWER

Yes. On very distributional hands the opponents may well stick their neck out and sacrifice themselves for a penalty hoping to stop you getting to the right slam. An extension to Blackwood will solve this problem. It's an acronym called DOPI.

DOUBLE = **0** Aces.   **P**ASS =   I Ace.

Next suit up shows 2 Aces etc.

HANDY HINTS

A successful suit slam requires a POWERFUL combination;

The POWER of High Card Points.

The POWER of Distribution.

The POWER of Trumps.

The POWER of Controls.

By the way, what exactly is a CONTROL?

You are about to find out!

(B) ELEMENTARY CUE BIDDING

If you are heading for a slam the Blackwood convention is ideal for discovering the NUMBER of Aces and Kings the partnership possesses. However, occasionally it is necessary to be able to discover the location of a SPECIFIC Ace or King.

e.g.

WEST	EAST
♠ 2	♠ Q765
♡ AKJ65	♡ Q987
◇ 43	◇ AQ6
♣ AKQ54	♣ J9

Six Hearts is a fantastic contract because the defence are only able to cash their Ace of Spades in defence. West can ultimately trump his losing diamond after East's diamonds have been thrown away on West's winning clubs.

Blackwood would have told West about the possession of an Ace in the East hand, but had it been the Ace of spades the defence would have been able to beat the slam by taking their Ace and King of diamonds!

You were advised at the start of the last chapter that the Blackwood convention was not generally suitable for hands containing a void. Add to this another gem.

RULE

Blackwood should NEVER be used on hands where you cannot guarantee that between you the partnership holds a first or second round control in EVERY suit.

A control can be an ACE; a KING; a SINGLETON; or a VOID.

If this rule is obeyed it will at least ensure that your slam will not flounder just because the defence have a cashing Ace and King in the same suit.

CUE BIDDING can be introduced into auctions to solve this problem and will often be used in conjunction with Blackwood. It may be classified as an advanced topic but I would be failing in my duty if I did not at least make you aware of this major problem associated with slam bidding even at this early stage of your bridge-playing life. I'll attempt to keep it simple. When you are ready to progress you can refer to a number of books on the market which specialise in this area. *(Step-by-Step: Slam Bidding – Alan Mould)*

Cue bids are usually made at the four or five level by bidding a new suit once a trump suit has been agreed.

Cue bidding auctions highlight the suit where a control is held and where a control is required.

Controls are shown in suit-ascending order. An Ace or void is a FIRST round control. A King or singleton is a SECOND round control. There is no priority.

Cue bidding sequences are used to elicit specific data which Blackwood cannot provide. Unfortunate though it may sometimes appear, cue bidding is not designed to give gratuitous information to the opponents about the strengths and weaknesses of all your suits.

Let's see how it works on the first example shown.

WEST	EAST
♠ 2	♠ Q765
♡ AKJ65	♡ Q987
◇ 43	◇ AQ6
♣ AKQ54	♣ J9

1♡	3♡
4♣	4◇
4NT	5◇
6♡	

West is in charge of the auction.

Lacking two controls in diamonds Blackwood is not on the menu – just yet. Having agreed hearts as trumps East knows the bid of Four Clubs is a cue bid showing a control in that suit. It does not promise a club suit. What does East do now? The Ace of Diamonds control should now be shown with a cue bid of Four Diamonds. It does not show a diamond suit. This is all the encouragement West needs to check on the number of Aces before bidding the slam. This is still necessary because it is conceivable that East cue bid a second round diamond control – a singleton or the King, and there might be two Aces missing.

Using the same example see what happens when West's diamonds and spades are interchanged.

WEST	EAST
♠ 43	♠ Q765
♡ AKJ65	♡ Q987
♢ 2	♢ AQ6
♣ AKQ54	♣ J9

1♡	3♡
4♣	4♢
4♡	Pass

The auction starts as before and again East co-operates by cue bidding his Ace of Diamonds. This does not excite West because he still has two key cards missing in the spade suit. By returning to the trump suit East will correctly draw the inference that his partner was looking for a control in spades and pass.

Change East's hand to;

♠ KQ7	♡ Q987	♢ A876	♣ 32

or

♠ 7	♡ Q987	♢ AK65	♣ J932

and he must continue the auction with a cue bid of Four Spades even though superficially it appears that West has 'signed off' in game. Further cue bidding would not now be necessary as West can safely continue by using Blackwood.

THE GRAND SLAM FORCE

It may not have escaped your notice that you cannot cue bid controls in the trump suit.

With Blackwood and cue bidding there to stop you reaching the stratosphere without a safety net, where is your guarantee to keep you out of a slam with a poor trump combination?

For the purposes of bidding a small slam – well, there isn't one. Judgement and luck are the only weapons you have at this level. The only good news in the trump department is for hands which are good enough to attempt a grand slam. Now it is crucial to own all three of the top trump honours.

Known as a GSF a bid of 5NT – which has not been preceded by 4NT – asks about the top three honours in the agreed trump suit.

i.e. the   ACE; KING; QUEEN

RESPONSES

BID 7 OF THE TRUMP SUIT WITH 2 HONOURS

BID 6 OF THE TRUMP SUIT WITH 1 HONOUR

BID 6♣ WITH 0 HONOUR

(If clubs are the agreed suit 6♣ = 0 OR 1 HONOUR)

EXAMPLE HANDS:

WEST	(a) EAST	(b) EAST
♠ KJ10876	♠ Q954	♠ AQ95
♡ AKQ53	♡ J2	♡ J2
◊ AK	◊ Q32	◊ Q32
♣ -	♣ KJ42	♣ KJ42

auction for hand (a)   auction for hand (b)

WEST	EAST	WEST	EAST
2♠	3♠	2♠	3♠
5NT	6♠	5NT	7♠

POINT TO PONDER

Missing one Ace should not prevent you from bidding a small slam any more than having all the Aces should encourage you to look for a grand slam. In fact you shouldn't really use the Blackwood convention unless you are prepared to bid a slam missing one Ace.

(C) QUANTITATIVE BIDDING

... for balanced hands.

No Trump contracts are deprived of the luxury of trumping losers. Unlike a trump contract hands played in No Trumps are not primarily concerned with discarding losers. Where there is no trump suit the route to success focuses entirely on being able to generate sufficient winners.

You are already familiar with the requirements to bid a slam in a suit contract. Unbalanced hands have a particular penchant to be played in a trump contract for reasons previously mentioned. By contrast, balanced hands do not generally benefit from nominating a trump suit.

While it is perfectly feasible to bring home a suit slam with as few as 20 HCP – obviously based on a particularly violent distribution – there is little scope for two balanced hands to produce 12 tricks without a stack of honour cards between them.

RULE

33 HCP are required to attempt 6NT

37 HCP are required to attempt 7NT

How do you set about discovering your combined point range?

Earlier chapters on opening and rebidding No Trumps taught you how to locate the 25 HCP required for game. Do you recall the basic bidding sequence 1NT - 2NT? The 2NT bid asked partner to bid 3NT holding a maximum 14 HCP and to pass holding a minimum. Another way of phrasing that question would be to say;

"What quantity of points do you hold, partner?"

This is known as quantitative bidding.

A bid is said to be quantitative when a direct raise of the same strain is enquiring about a point range.

Quantitative bids are always natural and limited. Apart from the very rare response of 5NT to a 1NT or 2NT opening bid, they are also non-forcing.

SUMMARY TABLE FOR QUANTITATIVE BIDDING IN NO TRUMPS

... where there is no interest in finding a trump fit.

Opening	Response	HCP	Message
1NT 12-14	2NT	11-12	Pass = MIN 3NT = MAX
	3NT	13-18	To play
	4NT	19-20	Pass = MIN 6NT = MAX
	5NT	23-24	6NT = MIN 7NT = MAX
	6NT	21-22	To play
	7NT	25-28	To play
2NT 20-22	3NT	4-10	To play
	4NT	11-12	Pass = MIN 6NT = MAX
	5NT	15-16	6NT = MIN 7NT = MAX
	6NT	13-14	To play
	7NT	17-20	To play

Quantitative No Trump bids exist in other sequences where a direct raise may have been preceded by suit bids.

e.g.

    1♡ - 1♠   or   1♠ - 2♣   or   1♠ - 2♡
    1NT - 4NT   3NT - 4NT   2NT - 4NT

Strangely enough, quantitative auctions to 4NT are frequently misinterpreted even by experienced players. There is a misguided fear that reaching a slam without the aid of Blackwood will result in disaster.

How can I allay *your* fears? I'll start by stating the obvious. If you can be sure of you have the requisite 33 HCP for 6NT you cannot have two Aces missing! Similarly with 37 HCP between the two hands there will not be a cashing Ace in the opponents hands!

I may not be able to ensure your contract is now watertight – but neither can the use of Blackwood. You can have all the Aces and Kings in the pack, but that only makes eight tricks.

I cannot conclude this section without mentioning that there will be the odd occasion when partner has opened the bidding with 1NT or 2NT and all you need to know for your slam are the number of controls partner holds. If 4NT is quantitative what happens to Blackwood? Another gentleman called John Gerber came up with a solution.

Enter ... THE GERBER CONVENTION!

On such rare occasions when your hand is distributionally powerful enough to go it alone a bid of 4♣ in direct response to one of these two opening bids asks for Aces. In much the same way as Blackwood the responses to Gerber are as follows;

4◊	=	0 or 4 Aces
4♡	=	1 Ace
4♠	=	2 Aces
4NT	=	3 Aces

Following the response to 4♣ a bid of 5♣ asks for Kings;

5◊	=	0 Kings
5♡	=	1 King
5♠	=	2 Kings
5NT	=	3 Kings
6♣	=	4 Kings

RULE

In similar fashion to the Blackwood principle, never ask for Kings when there is an Ace is missing.

This convention is not needed at any other time. A bid of 4♣ in any other situation will be either natural or a cue bid.

Chapter Eleven

COMPETITIVE BIDDING

Out in the real world auctions which do not attract interference from opponents are few and far between. Indeed, they are an open invitation to anyone who can afford to bid.

Your opponents may have started the bidding, but it would be wrong to presume, that for this reason, the final contract must belong to them. It is quite conceivable that your side has the balance of points or the distribution to make a game or even a slam. More frequently you will only be concerned with a partscore battle but you need to know the requirements for entering the fray.

Sometimes the auction you have initiated will be interrupted by an opponent's overcall. Sometimes it will be you or your partner who will perform this dastardly deed. Either way, you have to understand the strategy involved – from both sides of the table.

WHAT ARE THE BENEFITS OF COMPETING?

1. You might be able to make a contract.

2. Opening leads are often critical in determining the outcome of a contract. Your overcall will give partner direction if you end up defending.

3. Depriving the opponents of bidding space causes confusion. If you deny them a free run they might make the wrong decision.

4. You can force the opponents to compete to a higher level than they would have wished.

5. Opponents can be enticed into accepting a small penalty in exchange for what could have been a more lucrative plus score.

HOT TIP

Do not forget that the aim of the game is to get a plus score. Failing that, the smallest minus score.

As you can see, getting in on the action has much to recommend it though your enthusiasm must be tempered with judgement.

If you are not already fearful of entering the arena try this little conundrum …

… A hand which has the high card strength to open the bidding may lack the requirements to overcall, while a hand that is sub-minimum for an opening bid may exude sufficient playing strength to warrant an overcall!

YOUR OPTIONS IN THE LANGUAGE OF COMPETING INCLUDE:

☺   A SIMPLE OVERCALL

☺   A JUMP OVERCALL

☺   A INT OVERCALL

☺   A TAKEOUT DOUBLE

☺   A PENALTY DOUBLE

(A) A SIMPLE OVERCALL

When you open the bidding you announce approximately 12 HCP and your suit may be as poor as 5432. When you overcall in a suit the message is suit quality and distribution. High-card points are NOT necessarily the deciding factor.

A simple overcall describes a competitive bid made at the minimum level – i.e. without jumping the bidding.

At the one level your overcall can be on as few as 8 HCP while a two-level overcall is inadvisable with less than 10 HCP. Top of the range will rarely exceed 15 HCP, but keep an open mind for exceptional cases.

Suit quality is once again an overriding factor, but just as importantly you need at least a 5-card suit! Two-level overcalls are frequently punished with less than a 6-card suit. So BEWARE! There is a heavy price to pay for unruly behaviour in this department!

HOT TIP

While it is preferable to have a 6-card suit for a two-level overcall you can make an exception when the 5-card holding is strong and your hand is NOT a balanced 5-3-3-2 shape.

> **RULE**
>
> You require at least five cards in your overcalling suit but, in addition, suit quality is of the essence.

How is suit quality defined this time? Best advice now is to show you some examples to guide you.

EXAMPLE HANDS: Right-hand opponent opens 1♣. Do you overcall?

♠ AKJ63	♠ QJ65	♠ 83	♠ Q86432	♠ AQ43
♡ 72	♡ KQJ54	♡ 63	♡ 43	♡ 54
◇ 85	◇ 2	◇ K765	◇ 86	◇ AQ654
♣ 9642	♣ 753	♣ AK654	♣ AKJ	♣ 75
8 HCP	9 HCP	10 HCP	10 HCP	12 HCP
1♠	1♡	Pass	1♠	1◇

EXAMPLE HANDS: Right-hand opponent opens 1◇. Do you overcall?

♠ 85	♠ Q	♠ QJ983	♠ AQ2	♠ K8754
♡ AQ865	♡ J7	♡ AKQ63	♡ Q6	♡ J43
◇ 3	◇ KQ543	◇ 2	◇ KJ	◇ K
♣ K6543	♣ A7654	♣ 86	♣ 987653	♣ AQJ7
9 HCP	12 HCP	12 HCP	12 HCP	14 HCP
1♡	Pass	1♠	Pass	1♠

EXAMPLE HANDS: Right-hand opponent opens 1♡. Do you overcall?

♠ A109432	♠ KQJ4	♠ AJ54	♠ K8765	♠ Q5
♡ 9	♡ 2	♡ Q7654	♡ AK543	♡ Q8
◇ J32	◇ KQJ654	◇ K6	◇ 6	◇ KQJ
♣ K65	♣ 43	♣ K4	♣ A5	♣ AJ7654
8 HCP	12 HCP	13 HCP	14 HCP	15 HCP
1♠	2◇	Pass!	1♠	2♣

With a low point count a 5-card suit will be headed by two top honours. Holding a longer suit or a stronger hand you can be much more flexible.

If you are dealt two 5-card suits choose to overcall the higher-ranking suit with a view to bidding the other one on the next round. The level to which you are prepared to compete will be greatly influenced by the general strength of the hand.

Occasionally your opponents will open the bidding in your longest suit! Pass for now and lie in wait unless you happen to have another suit of at least five cards in which you are strong enough to compete.

Having made your initial contribution to the auction one awaits developments.

Put yourself on the other side of the table ...

RESPONSES TO A SIMPLE OVERCALL

The beauty of promising a 5-card suit for an overcall means that as their partner you only need three of them to support. There is absolutely no need for you to vie with your partner to be the declarer — especially if a major suit has been suggested — unless you have something a lot better in mind.

Despite the incredibly wide range for the overcall coupled with the fact there may be as few as 8 HCP lurking in partner's hand your range of responses are relatively straight forward.

(1) If you can support partner's suit the level to which you raise is comparable to a response of an opening bid.

A raise to the two level	=	6-9 HCP
A raise to the three level	=	10-12 HCP
A raise to game	=	13+ HCP

With four or more cards in support you should be a little more aggressive in competition and consider the merits of crossing the boundaries of these zones.

(2) Responding in No Trumps requires a much stronger hand than a normal response and, needless to say, a stopper in the opponent's suit.

AFTER A ONE-LEVEL OVERCALL;

1NT	=	8-11 HCP
2NT	=	12-14 HCP
3NT	=	15+ HCP

AFTER A TWO-LEVEL OVERCALL;

2NT	=	10-12 HCP
3NT	=	13+ HCP

(3) Changing the suit is your last option. Nondescript hands with minimal values – say up to 8 HCP – should pass. Facing a simple overcall game is unlikely and if you have not got a fit or a very good 6-card suit you are probably too high already!

Introducing a new suit, therefore, suggests better things may lie ahead. The message is clearly constructive though not forcing and will promise at least a 5-card suit. To force a response from partner you must make a jump shift.

EXAMPLE HANDS: Left-hand opponent opens 1♣. Partner overcalls 1♡. Right-hand opponent passes. How do you respond?

♠ J765	♠ K876	♠ QJ2	♠ A865	♠ KJ5
♡ 8	♡ K65	♡ 53	♡ QJ65	♡ 74
◇ K653	◇ 532	◇ Q987	◇ K63	◇ AQ54
♣ Q532	♣ 974	♣ KJ87	♣ 43	♣ QJ98
6 HCP	6 HCP	9 HCP	10 HCP	13 HCP
Pass	2♡	1NT	3♡	2NT

EXAMPLE HANDS: Left-hand opponent opens 1◊. Partner overcalls 1♠. Right-hand opponent passes. How do you respond?

♠ K7	♠ QJ876	♠ 3	♠ 42	♠ J5
♡ K8765	♡ A9876	♡ AKJ765	♡ KQJ	♡ A54
◊ 6543	◊ 3	◊ Q43	◊ AQJ2	◊ K3
♣ J4	♣ A5	♣ J76	♣ Q765	♣ AK9876
7 HCP	11 HCP	11 HCP	15 HCP	15 HCP
Pass	4♠	2♡	3NT	3♣

EXAMPLE HANDS: Left-hand opponent opens 1♡. Partner overcalls 2♣. Right-hand opponent passes. How do you respond?

♠ 8765	♠ Q964	♠ AK765	♠ AQJ763	♠ Q43
♡ 98	♡ AJ8	♡ 87	♡ 954	♡ K763
◊ A432	◊ K76	◊ AJ765	◊ K5	◊ Q65
♣ KQ4	♣ J43	♣ 2	♣ K5	♣ AQ2
9 HCP	11 HCP	12 HCP	13 HCP	13 HCP
3♣	2NT	2♠	3♠	3NT

POINT TO PONDER

The philosophy of defensive bidding will become more meaningful with experience. Finding a fit early on in a competitive auction gives you the momentum to obstruct the enemy.

(B) A JUMP OVERCALL

Picture a hand with 11-15 HCP and a decent 6 or 7-card suit and you have the ingredients for an intermediate SINGLE JUMP OVERCALL. It can be defined more accurately as a one-suited hand of opening bid strength with a minimum but sound rebid.

EXAMPLE HANDS: Right-hand opponent opens 1◊. How do you overcall?

♠ KQJ976	♠ K4	♠ AQ2	♠ A86543	♠ J64
♡ AJ3	♡ AQJ765	♡ J4	♡ AJ76	♡ 2
◊ 943	◊ 96	◊ K3	◊ Q7	◊ KQJ
♣ 2	♣ Q86	♣ Q98543	♣ K	♣ AKJ864
11 HCP	12 HCP	12 HCP	14 HCP	15 HCP
2♠	2♡	2♣	1♠	3♣

EXAMPLE HANDS: Right-hand opponent opens 1♡. How do you overcall?

♠ AJ5432	♠ 2	♠ Q8	♠ AKQ543	♠ A32
♡ 8	♡ A65	♡ Q4	♡ 765	♡ KQ8765
◊ KQJ3	◊ AKJ984	◊ A3	◊ QJ	◊ J4
♣ 54	♣ 876	♣ KQJ8765	♣ K4	♣ AJ
11 HCP	12 HCP	14 HCP	15 HCP	15 HCP
1♠	3◊	3♣	2♠	Pass!

HOT TIP

If your jump overcall forces you to bid at the three level it is considerably safer to be at the upper end of your range if you are vulnerable.

No doubt you are now wondering just how high you can actually overcall! Recalling Chapter Eight on preempts you were able to open the bidding at the three level with just 6-10 HCP if you had a robust 7-card suit. The same criteria applies to making a DOUBLE JUMP OVERCALL but please ...

(a) Ensure you ARE now making a DOUBLE JUMP and

(b) Don't forget about suit quality!

Should your preemptive overcall force you to bid at the four level, even greater playing strength is expressed. Frequently possessing a top-quality 8-card suit it denies the defensive strength associated with a normal opening bid at the one or two level.

EXAMPLE HANDS: Right-hand opponent opens 1♢. How do you overcall?

♠ AKJ7543	♠ 2	♠ Q2	♠ AKQJ8765	♠ J5
♡ 32	♡ KQJ8754	♡ Q2	♡ 2	♡ 3
♢ J64	♢ 432	♢ AQ65432	♢ 8	♢ 53
♣ 4	♣ 73	♣ 86	♣ J54	♣ AQJ98765
9 HCP	6 HCP	10 HCP	11 HCP	8 HCP
3♠	3♡	Pass!	4♠	4♣

EXAMPLE HANDS: Right-hand opponent opens 1♠. How do you overcall?

♠ 43	♠ J64	♠ 2	♠ A8	♠ Q
♡ KQJ6543	♡ 2	♡ KQJ6	♡ KQJ87542	♡ J3
♢ 95	♢ AQJ76543	♢ 7	♢ 86	♢ J2
♣ 43	♣ 3	♣ KJ86542	♣ 8	♣ AK876543
6 HCP	8 HCP	10 HCP	10 HCP	11 HCP
Pass	4♢	2♣	4♡	4♣

RESPONSES TO A JUMP OVERCALL

It is no coincidence that every hand deemed suitable for an intermediate jump overcall has the power to muster at least six tricks if it can get to choose trumps.

This factor alone should influence your judgement in deciding the final contract. If you are strong enough for game perhaps nine tricks in No Trumps will be easier than ten in a major. Food for thought. With a long suit to run marginal decisions should definitely err on the side of aggression especially when a 3NT game is in the frame.

EXAMPLE HANDS: Left-hand opponent opens 1♣. Partner overcalls 2♡. Right-hand opponent passes. How do you respond?

♠ K54	♠ KJ53	♠ 4	♠ AK987	♠ QJ76
♡ 32	♡ 4	♡ J765	♡ 2	♡ K74
◊ Q9863	◊ Q987	◊ AQ765	◊ KQ973	◊ QJ3
♣ J64	♣ KJ97	♣ A65	♣ 74	♣ AJ9
6 HCP	10 HCP	11 HCP	12 HCP	14 HCP
Pass	2NT	4♡	2♠	3NT!

EXAMPLE HANDS: Left-hand opponent opens 1♠. Partner overcalls 3♣. Right-hand opponent passes. How do you respond?

♠ J753	♠ QJ4	♠ 43	♠ 76	♠ A2
♡ Q763	♡ J7654	♡ AKJ76	♡ KQ	♡ 5
◊ AJ862	◊ A54	◊ K965	◊ KQJ7	◊ AK9876
♣ -	♣ K3	♣ J2	♣ Q8653	♣ A432
8 HCP	11 HCP	12 HCP	13 HCP	15 HCP
Pass	3NT	3♡	5♣	4NT

RULE

A change of suit (that isn't a game bid) is forcing for one round.

RULE

A raise of partner's suit to the three level is also a try for game, but only requires 2-card support.

Now try responding to a DOUBLE JUMP overcall;

EXAMPLE HANDS: Left-hand opponent opens 1♣. Partner overcalls 3♡. Right-hand opponent passes. How do you respond?

♠ 876	♠ KJ76	♠ AJ7	♠ AKQ876	♠ A54
♡ KJ7	♡ 2	♡ Q54	♡ 5	♡ A54
◊ A432	◊ Q876	◊ A65	◊ A654	◊ KQJ76
♣ 974	♣ KJ76	♣ QJ43	♣ J5	♣ 87
8 HCP	10 HCP	14 HCP	14 HCP	14 HCP
4♡!	Pass!	3NT	3♠	4♡

HOT TIP

Recognising the difference between an intermediate jump overcall and a weaker preemptive manoeuvre will be your biggest test! It may seem trivial now but at-the-table experiences can do funny things to your bridge hormones!

(C) A 1NT OVERCALL

In complete contrast to overcalling a suit with as few as 8 HCP a balanced hand requires careful handling. After an opening bid by the opponents it is considered dangerous to enter the auction with this shaped hand unless it is very strong. Hence, you need even more points to overcall with 1NT than for an opening bid of the same.

It is customary to play a 1NT overcall to show 15-18 HCP plus a stop in the opponent's suit. Holding a weaker, balanced hand you are advised to pass on the first round — unless you can show a decent 5-card suit at the one level — even though you may have sufficient values to open the bidding.

EXAMPLE HANDS: Right-hand opponent opens 1♦. Do you overcall?

♠ AJ65	♠ K65	♠ J7643	♠ Q8	♠ KQ2
♡ KQ5	♡ A2	♡ KJ6	♡ AKJ76	♡ A8765
◊ KQ2	◊ Q65	◊ AQ2	◊ 975	◊ KQ5
♣ 987	♣ KQJ65	♣ AJ	♣ AQ5	♣ K4
15 HCP	15 HCP	16 HCP	16 HCP	17 HCP
1NT	1NT	1NT	1♡	1NT

EXAMPLE HANDS: Right-hand opponent opens 1♡. Do you overcall?

♠ J8	♠ KQJ65	♠ A43	♠ QJ6	♠ AJ
♡ QJ65	♡ J5	♡ AKJ	♡ KJ8	♡ AQ
◊ KQJ6	◊ AK6	◊ Q432	◊ AJ972	◊ K8763
♣ KJ4	♣ J63	♣ Q98	♣ KQ	♣ A432
14 HCP	15 HCP	16 HCP	17 HCP	18 HCP
Pass	1♠	1NT	1NT	1NT

RESPONSES TO A 1NT OVERCALL

This section just couldn't be easier! Imagine partner has opened the bidding with 1NT and reply as usual BUT ...

... remember to adjust your point range to accommodate the extra strength shown!

SUMMARY TABLE FOR RESPONDING TO A 1NT OVERCALL		
(a)	=	0-6 HCP.
PASS	=	To play.
2♣	=	Stayman convention.
2◇ 2♡ 2♠	=	Weak take out. 5+ card suit.
(b)	=	7-8 HCP.
2♣	=	Stayman convention.
2NT	=	Balanced invitation to 3NT.
(c) =		9+ HCP.
2♣	=	Stayman convention.
3♣ 3◇	=	6+ card suit. Forcing to at least game.
3♡ 3♠	=	5-card suit. Asking for 3+ support.
3NT	=	To play.
4♡ 4♠	=	6+ card suit. To play.

EXAMPLE HANDS: Left-hand opponent opens 1◇. Partner overcalls 1NT. Right-hand opponent passes. How do you respond?

♠ J7654	♠ K432	♠ Q63	♠ K82	♠ 842
♡ 32	♡ Q7532	♡ A72	♡ Q87	♡ KJ743
◇ 863	◇ 97	◇ 96	◇ 852	◇ Q3
♣ 732	♣ 42	♣ Q5432	♣ KJ73	♣ A62
1 HCP	5 HCP	8 HCP	9 HCP	10 HCP
2♠	2♣	2NT	3NT	3♡

(D) DOUBLES

In addition to the normal bids available to you in an auction you can choose to say "DOUBLE". You can only ever double your opponent's call – not your partner's!

There are two main uses for the double.

THE TAKEOUT DOUBLE

Your right-hand opponent opens the bidding with 1♡. What action could you take if you held?

> ♠ AQ76
> ♡ 3
> ♢ KQ65
> ♣ J907

To overcall with a suit you need at least a 5-carder. To overcall 1NT you require 15-18 HCP – not to mention a stop in hearts. This hand does not meet any of these requirements.

> ### RULE
>
> If you double an opponent's suit at the one, two or three level when partner has not shown any points it is a TAKEOUT DOUBLE.

This is simply a request for partner to choose the trump suit and initially shows a hand that is short of THEIR suit, but has adequate support for any of the unbid suits. The above hand is a perfect example of a double after an opponent has bid hearts.

> ### RULE
>
> A takeout double promises the values for an opening bid with no upper point limit.

Ideally your shape will be 4-4-4-1; 4-4-3-2; 5-4-4-0; or occasionally 5-4-3-1; with the shortage ALWAYS being in the opponent's suit – but prefer to overcall a good 5-card major rather than make a takeout double.

EXAMPLE HANDS:
Your right-hand opponent opens 1♣. How do you overcall?

♠ KJ75	♠ Q732	♠ Q32	♠ KQJ76	♠ AQ4
♡ A876	♡ QJ74	♡ KQJ3	♡ AK654	♡ KQ62
◇ K765	◇ 7	◇ AQ73	◇ Q2	◇ KJ65
♣ 2	♣ AK43	♣ 87	♣ J	♣ K4
11 HCP	12 HCP	14 HCP	16 HCP	18 HCP
Double	Pass	Double	1♠	1NT

HOT TIP

Do not use the double if your hand is best decribed with a natural overcall.

Natural overcalls, however, are limited. What happens if your hand exceeds the expected HCP range for one of those bids? ...

... DOUBLE comes to the rescue!

With a hand that is too strong for either a simple overcall, a jump overcall, or a 1NT overcall a different strategy is called for.

Start with a double. The plan is to await a response from your partner and then complete the picture of your hand at your next turn to call.

EXAMPLE HANDS:
Your right-hand opponent opens 1◇. How do you overcall?

♠ AJ7	♠ A76	♠ KQJ	♠ KQ6	♠ AK2
♡ QJ2	♡ 76	♡ A2	♡ KQ32	♡ AKJ876
◇ 5	◇ KQ76	◇ 6	◇ AQ6	◇ A4
♣ KJ8764	♣ KQ54	♣ AQJ8765	♣ K73	♣ 98
12 HCP	14 HCP	17 HCP	19 HCP	19 HCP
2♣	Pass	Double	Double	Double

EXAMPLE HANDS:

Your right-hand opponent opens 1♡. How do you overcall?

♠ AKJ65	♠ J52	♠ K765	♠ AQJ864	♠ AJ6
♡ K76	♡ KQ2	♡ 2	♡ AK	♡ KJ7
◇ 8	◇ AK	◇ AK83	◇ KQJ5	◇ AKJ6
♣ J752	♣ KQ543	♣ AKJ5	♣ 4	♣ A75
12 HCP	18 HCP	18 HCP	20 HCP	21 HCP
1♠	1NT	Double	Double	Double

A takeout double is not confined to the overcaller in 2nd position. You can double after both opponents have bid and still convey a similar message.

e.g.

North	East	South	West
1♡	Pass	2♡	Dble

In this sequence double is takeout of hearts promising an opening bid plus support for the three unbid suits.

♠ KQ42
♡ J
◇ AQJ8
♣ J732

e.g.

North	East	South	West
1♣	Pass	1♠	Dble

In this sequence double shows at least 4 diamonds and 4 hearts plus opening bid values.

♠ Q32
♡ AKQ5
◇ KJ82
♣ 76

Of course the doubler may be concealing one of those strong varieties of hands – in which case all will be revealed on the next round.

GOLDEN RULES FOR A TAKEOUT DOUBLE

1. Partner has not bid to indicate any values.

2. A takeout double requires a certain combination of HCP and distribution. You need one of the following 3 hand types.

HAND TYPE A
An opening hand of 11+ HCP with a shortage in the enemy suit plus support for the unbid suits.

HAND TYPE B
A hand which is too strong for a suit overcall with 16+ HCP.

HAND TYPE C
A balanced hand which is too strong for a 1NT overcall with 19+ HCP.

RESPONSES TO A TAKEOUT DOUBLE

Your worst nightmare has come true. Partner has made a takeout double and you do not have any points. Do not panic!

The responses to a takeout double really do cater for these situations. After all it's hardly your fault if you were not dealt any points!

RULE

For the purposes of *responding* to a takeout double you must assume that partner is holding HAND TYPE A: an opening hand of 11+ HCP with a shortage in the enemy suit plus support for the unbid suits.

The reason for this is simply because it is the most common hand type of the three. It houses the only weak option together with an extensive point range and thus requires maximum co-operation. The stronger hands are more self-sufficient and have a pretty good indication of where they're heading.

If your right-hand opponent passes partner's double use one of the following options to describe your hand:

BID A NEW SUIT AT SIMPLE LEVEL   0-7 HCP
Pick the longest of the other three suits or the major with equal length.
Occasionally you will be forced to bid a 3-card suit.

BID A NEW SUIT BY JUMPING ONE LEVEL   8-11 HCP
Pick the longest of the other three suits or the major with equal length. This
is a try for game if partner is not minimum.

BID A NEW SUIT AT GAME LEVEL   12+ HCP
Pick the game in which you would like to play.

BID THE OPPONENT'S SUIT   12+ HCP
Use this bid to put the ball back in partner's court. You either have a choice
of game bids or your hand is strong enough to suggest a slam.

PASS!   6+ HCP
Far from being a sign of weakness it shows length and strength in the
opponent's suit. Conversion to a penalty is based on a VERY STRONG
TRUMP HOLDING; e.g. KQJ98 of their suit and commands a trump lead –
if partner has one!

BID NO TRUMPS   6-15 HCP
With a less robust holding in the opponent's suit, but nevertheless promising
at least one stop, it may be more appropriate to suggest a No Trump
contract.

1NT	=	6-9 HCP
2NT	=	10-12 HCP
3NT	=	13-15 HCP

EXAMPLE HANDS:
Your left-hand opponent opens 1♣. Partner doubles.
Right-hand opponent passes. How do you respond?

♠ 9876	♠ 863	♠ AJ864	♠ 32	♠ AQ43
♡ 432	♡ J84	♡ 86	♡ 765	♡ AQ43
◇ 543	◇ J63	◇ K4	◇ K4	◇ 76
♣ 864	♣ AQ73	♣ J765	♣ KQJ876	♣ J32
0 HCP	8 HCP	9 HCP	9 HCP	13 HCP
1♠	1NT	2♠	PASS	2♣!

EXAMPLE HANDS:

Your left-hand opponent opens 1♡. Partner doubles.
Right-hand opponent passes. How do you respond?

♠ 974	♠ 983	♠ K43	♠ Q2	♠ KJ987
♡ 5432	♡ J65	♡ J65	♡ KQJ2	♡ AJ4
◇ 642	◇ 732	◇ AQ852	◇ KJ5	◇ QJ54
♣ 864	♣ K876	♣ J3	♣ 5432	♣ 2
0 HCP	4 HCP	11 HCP	12 HCP	12 HCP
1♠!	2♣	3◇	2NT	4♠

When your right-hand opponent makes a natural bid instead of passing, your obligation to respond has been removed because partner will always get another chance to bid. Hence, you should only bid when you can make a positive contribution to the auction.

And so it's back to the doubler ...

DOUBLER REBIDS

Not wishing to complicate the doubling process for you unnecessarily there is still some important groundwork to cover before you can feel confident of using it.

> ### RULE
>
> If partner has passed the double, that will probably end the auction. Lead a trump – if you have one. Partner has not converted your takeout double out of weakness. It is a sign of length and strength in the opponent's suit. By attacking trumps you can significantly reduce declarer's trick-taking potential.

If you have **HAND TYPE A** and partner has picked a trump suit at the minimum level possible showing 0-7 HCP your rebid will fall into one of these point bands;

11-15 HCP	-	Pass
16-18 HCP	-	Raise one level
19-20 HCP	-	Raise two levels
21+ HCP	-	Bid game

Having said all this it is vital to be flexible within these ranges. Your choice of rebid may well be influenced by whether partner has picked a minor or a major. With a strong hand which could be more successful in a No Trump game one can bid the opponent's suit to request a stop in that suit.

If partner has jumped the bidding to show 8-11 HCP this indicates interest in a game opposite a non-minimum double. Depending on the trump fit and the general overall strength of your hand one should accept with 15+ HCP. Again, you can use a bid of the opponent's suit to explore for a game in No Trumps.

If the response to your takeout double was a number of No Trumps your next bid will be governed by your strength and shape.

Holding **HAND TYPE B** you will simply pick your own trump suit. The message should be clear to partner that you now have 16+ HCP and a hand that was far too strong for a normal overcall. If partner's initial response has indicated 8 or more HCP your call will be forcing to game, but if you want to keep the auction alive opposite 0-7 HCP you will have to jump the bidding.

HAND TYPE C is strong and balanced, neatly described with a rebid in No Trumps. With 19-21 HCP you should bid them at the LOWEST AVAILABLE LEVEL, reserving a jump in No Trumps for hands with 22 or more HCP.

EXAMPLE HANDS:
Your right-hand opponent opened 1◊. You doubled.
Partner has responded (a) 1♣; (b) 3♣; What do you bid next?

♠ KQ65	♠ AJ52	♠ K7	♠ KQ3	♠ AK32
♡ Q864	♡ AK73	♡ AKQ654	♡ AJ87	♡ QJ3
◊ 3	◊ 63	◊ J7	◊ AQ2	◊ J
♣ AK43	♣ KJ2	♣ A32	♣ K92	♣ AKJ87
14 HCP	16 HCP	17 HCP	19 HCP	19 HCP
(a) Pass	2♠	2♡	1NT!	3♠
(b) Pass	3◊!	3♡	3NT	5♣

EXAMPLE HANDS:
Your right-hand opponent opened 1♡. You doubled.
Partner has responded (a) 1NT; (b) 2◇; What do you bid next?

♠ K974	♠ AQJ987	♠ QJ74	♠ A987	♠ AJ6
♡ -	♡ KJ5	♡ 92	♡ 8	♡ KJ7
◇ KQJ2	◇ A2	◇ AKQ3	◇ KQJ7	◇ AKJ6
♣ Q7654	♣ J5	♣ KQ6	♣ AKQ2	♣ A75
11 HCP	16 HCP	17 HCP	19 HCP	21 HCP
(a) Pass	2♠	2NT	3NT	3NT
(b) Pass	2♠	3◇	2♡!	2NT

In earlier chapters I drummed in the necessity to locate the magic combination of 25 HCP before attempting game, yet now we seem to be throwing caution to the wind.

Distributional features frequently allow you to overrule those cherished words of wisdom ...

... and so the saga goes on.

Declaring with a shortage in the opponent's bid suit greatly diminishes the enemy's defensive powers while enhancing your own playing strength.

Your success as a declarer often depends on guessing the whereabouts of key cards, or discovering the opposition's distribution. So, if you do become declarer after an opponent has bid – either because they have opened or overcalled – your task has surely been simplified.

HOT TIP

Armed with so much extra knowledge you should always consider the merits of bidding a game in a competitive auction even when you know your side may have slightly less than 25 HCP.

HANDY HINTS

Natural overcalls are not forcing even if you jump the bidding.

A shortage means two or fewer cards.

Don't ask partner to pick the trump suit if you would rather pick it yourself! – unless you are very strong.

Remember, partner has not promised any points when responding to a double.

POINT TO PONDER

Competing has drawbacks too. Overcalling ground can conceal a minefield of traps. For one thing, there is a real danger of conceding a frivolous penalty. For another, information will be given gratuitously to the enemy concerning your shape and strength which will inevitably be used to their advantage if they declare. Be cautious when YOU decide to overcall.

Frustration may set in occasionally when you are dealt an opening bid but lack the criteria for an overcall. You may need a poker face too when an opponent has had the effrontery to open the bidding with YOUR best suit! The penultimate section of this chapter is all about PROTECTIVE BIDDING which is designed to get you back into the auction on good hands where you or your partner originally passed ...

... but first, a brief introduction to the PENALTY DOUBLE.

THE PENALTY DOUBLE

Just as the name suggests a penalty double seeks extra scoring points in defence when a contract does not make.

If a takeout double requests partner to take out the last bid into another contract then a penalty double does the opposite. It says to partner *"Do not take this double out as I do not think their contract will make"*.

Of course you do have rights! No one can force you not to bid – it is merely a very strong suggestion that your best chance of a plus score will come from defending rather than declaring. Sometimes partner is wrong, but common sense usually prevails when you are in need of guidance.

If a double of a suit bid at the one, two or three level is defined as takeout, when do penalty doubles surface? The answer to this question will be covered in depth very shortly in Chapter Twelve. However, what I do want to tell you now is that a double of a 1NT opening bid is for PENALTIES.

For this manoeuvre you will require a minimum of 15 HCP. Having said that, the rules of this game, as you know, are constantly being broken. Hopefully these example hands will explain when and why as well as serve to reinforce the requirements for a two-level overcall.

EXAMPLE HANDS:
Your right-hand opponent opens 1NT. How do you overcall?

♠ KQJ6	♠ AK642	♠ 54	♠ KJ4	♠ 2
♡ A75	♡ Q5	♡ A	♡ Q86	♡ AKJ7
◇ K42	◇ KQJ3	◇ AKJ75	◇ AQJ32	◇ QJ76
♣ J52	♣ 83	♣ AJ643	♣ AQ	♣ AKQ3
14 HCP	15 HCP	17 HCP	19 HCP	20 HCP
Pass	Double	Double	Double	Double

EXAMPLE HANDS:
Your right-hand opponent opens 1NT. How do you overcall?

♠ Q65	♠ AQJ76	♠ KQJ65	♠ 93	♠ J98
♡ KQ4	♡ 5	♡ Q2	♡ 65	♡ KQJ98
◇ AJ9876	◇ KQ84	◇ K64	◇ A3	◇ AQ2
♣ 2	♣ J42	♣ QJ5	♣ AKQJ764	♣ K4
12 HCP	13 HCP	14 HCP	14 HCP	16 HCP
2◇	2♠	Pass	Double	Double

(E) PROTECTIVE BIDDING

Leaving your opponents to play peacefully in a low-level contract may be a friendly gesture, but it rarely produces a satisfactory result for your side.

The lower their contract the more likely it is that (a) they will make it and (b) you have sufficient resources to make a contract your way.

The art of competing is cultivated through experience. Judgement will play a large role in determining your success in this area.

For my part I can at least give you some pointers and show you HOW to compete, but WHEN …? That is where you will have to work hard and learn to LISTEN TO THE BIDDING.

Every hand you will ever play has a PROTECTOR. This is the player who has the ability to keep the auction alive for at least another round or end proceedings. The topic of protective bidding, however, is more commonly associated with an auction that is about to be passed out at the one level.

PROTECTING IN THE FOURTH SEAT

i.e. Left-hand opponent opens with a suit at the one level and the next two players PASS.

Most of the time the normal rules for overcalling will still apply even in 4th seat. That is to say you need a 5-card suit to bid at the one level, preferably a 6-card suit to overcall at the two level and the qualifications for a jump overcall also remain the same. Even a takeout double carries the same meaning. So what exactly is different?

There are THREE big rule changes.

RULE ONE

A bid of 1NT in the 4th seat shows a balanced hand with 11-14 HCP and does NOT promise a stop in the opponent's suit.

RULE TWO

A bid of 2NT in the 4th seat shows a balanced hand and 19-21 HCP.

RULE THREE

Your protective double can be made with as few as 10 HCP.

SUMMARY TABLE FOR PROTECTING IN FOURTH SEAT

1NT	=	11-14	HCP	=	Balanced. Stop not promised.
Double	=	10+	HCP	=	Expected ideal shape.
	=	15-18	HCP	=	Balanced. Will rebid NT's.
	=	22+	HCP	=	Balanced. Will jump in NT's.
	=	16+	HCP	=	Unbalanced. Will rebid suit.
2NT	=	19-21	HCP	=	Balanced with stop.
Simple Overcall	=	8-15 10-15	HCP HCP	=	5+ cards at one level. 6+ cards at two level.
Jump Overcall	=	11-15	HCP	=	6+ cards. Good quality suit.

EXAMPLE HANDS:

Left-hand opponent opens 1♣ followed by two passes. Your bid.

♠ KQ765	♠ QJ54	♠ AJ3	♠ K6	♠ KJ4
♡ 43	♡ AQ32	♡ J65	♡ AKQ642	♡ AQ3
◊ K76	◊ J432	◊ KQ32	◊ 64	◊ QJ762
♣ 432	♣ 7	♣ 973	♣ J43	♣ AQ
8 HCP	10 HCP	11 HCP	13 HCP	19 HCP
1♠	DOUBLE	1NT	2♡	2NT

EXAMPLE HANDS:

Left-hand opponent opens 1♡ followed by two passes. Your bid.

♠ AK84	♠ QJ2	♠ KQJ32	♠ AJ	♠ K54
♡ 4	♡ AJ98	♡ 32	♡ Q2	♡ K76
◊ K83	◊ J983	◊ AJ543	◊ K98743	◊ A2
♣ 98653	♣ Q2	♣ 2	♣ K65	♣ AKJ765
10 HCP	11 HCP	11 HCP	13 HCP	18 HCP
Double	1NT	1♠	2◊	Double

You may be wondering why it is OK to protect with 1NT holding as few as 11 HCP yet you need a super-strong hand to overcall 1NT in second position.

The answer lies in the question! Your partner may have been itching to bid with numerous hand-types that were worth an opening bid, but lacked the criteria to overcall. Most commonly that will be when s/he had a balanced hand with 12-14 HCP! Imagine partner holding one of those 14-point hands and you can see why it is imperative to protect with 11 HCP.

Other hand patterns which frustrate intervention include the occasions when opener has pinched partner's suit! A protective double from you might be just what the doctor ordered for a very healthy plus score your way.

RESPONSES TO PROTECTION IN THE FOURTH SEAT
The good news for responding to the protective 1NT is that you use EXACTLY the same methods as over a 1NT opening bid ignoring the possibility that occasionally partner may only have 11 HCP.

Your responses to a protective 2NT should be automatic too – if you have remembered everything from Chapter Seven.

Responding to a protective takeout double cannot be taken so lightly. Extra care is need in this position. Unlike the No Trump ranges used for responding to a second seat takeout double your ...

1NT response should combine both 6-9 HCP AND 10-12 HCP;

2NT requires 13-14 HCP;

3NT requires 15+ HCP

... all with robust stops in the enemy suit.

Similarly, jump responses made in a suit need to be measured more cautiously to compensate for the possibility of there being only 10 HCP to greet you.

EXAMPLE HANDS:

Right-hand opponent opens 1♣ followed by two passes. Partner bids (a) DOUBLE; (b) 1NT. RHO passes. What action do you take?

♠ 65	♠ J86	♠ K5	♠ KJ76	♠ Q53
♡ 86	♡ Q762	♡ A43	♡ A3	♡ 9876
◇ QJ765	◇ 87	◇ 7653	◇ K76	◇ KJ8
♣ J762	♣ Q432	♣ QJ76	♣ 8762	♣ AK3
4 HCP	5 HCP	10 HCP	11 HCP	13 HCP
(a) 1◇	1♡	1NT	2♠	2NT
(b) 2◇	Pass	Pass	2♣!	3NT

EXAMPLE HANDS:

Right-hand opponent opens 1♡ followed by two passes. Partner bids (a) 1♠; (b) 2NT. RHO passes. What action do you take?

♠ 32	♠ KJ987	♠ J764	♠ KJ2	♠ A865
♡ A74	♡ 43	♡ 5	♡ J6	♡ K765
◇ 864	◇ Q972	◇ 9753	◇ K654	◇ 42
♣ J7654	♣ 65	♣ AQ32	♣ 8642	♣ QJ2
5 HCP	6 HCP	7 HCP	8 HCP	10 HCP
(a) Pass	2♠	2♠	2♠	3♠
(b) 3NT	3♠	3♣!	3NT	3♣!

HOT TIP

If you become declarer when an opponent has freely passed their partner's opening bid remember that this player will have less than 6 HCP!

PROTECTING IN OTHER POSITIONS

As already stated the principle of protection can be used in any sequence where a 'PASS' will end the auction. This does not mean it is always safe to bid but, unquestionably, it pays to do your homework as early as possible during the auction and try to work out the likely distribution of HCP between the 4 hands – even if your side is yet to enter the auction!

EXAMPLE HANDS: You are EAST.

North	East	South	West
1♡	Pass	2♡	Pass
Pass	?		

♠ KJ76	♠ J9765	♠ J5	♠ Q863	♠ AK3
♡ 3	♡ K3	♡ 876	♡ 95	♡ KQJ9
◇ Q876	◇ J432	◇ KJ9876	◇ KQ3	◇ 6543
♣ K876	♣ A4	♣ A2	♣ QJ76	♣ J3
9 HCP	9 HCP	9 HCP	10 HCP	14 HCP
Double	2♠	3◇	Double	Pass!

EXAMPLE HANDS: You are WEST.

North	East	South	West
1♠	Pass	1NT	Pass
2♣	Pass	Pass	?

♠ K54	♠ 2	♠ 765	♠ Q2	♠ AK54
♡ KJ6	♡ AK54	♡ A2	♡ KQJ5	♡ J65
◇ J7	◇ J863	◇ A2	◇ 654	◇ K76
♣ J6543	♣ J765	♣ Q98765	♣ K432	♣ Q32
9 HCP	9 HCP	10 HCP	11 HCP	13 HCP
Pass	Double	3♣	Double	Pass!

Bidding after initially passing should not delude partner into thinking you forgot to bid on the last round!

HOT TIP

LISTENING TO THE BIDDING will not only help you make that vital decision in the protective seat, but will ultimately improve your awareness in defence.

POINT TO PONDER

Try not to punish partner for protecting 'light' because, in time to come, accurate bidding in the protective zone will determine your transition from being a beginner/improver to an advanced improver/expert!

(F) DEFENCE TO OPENING BIDS AT THE THREE LEVEL

Now that you are fully acquainted with the different ways in which you can compete, the time has come to discuss your defence to those irritating preemptive suit opening bids at the three level.

In essence you can overcall as if the bidding had started at the one level. Space, however, is limited and you will need to modify that strategy very slightly. Just as importantly your entrance into the auction is at a considerably higher level and you need to take out some insurance for this by having a little in reserve in case the fates are unkind.

YOUR OPTIONS

PASS!	-	You'll probably recognise one of these hands instinctively!
A SUIT OVERCALL	-	Unless particularly distributional, say 5-5, you will have at least a 6-card suit and 14+ HCP. Very strong unbalanced hands can jump directly to game or start by doubling.
DOUBLE	-	Takeout. 14+ HCP with a shortage in the opponent's suit and support for the three unbid suits.
3NT	-	Balanced with a stop in the opening suit and – wait for it – 16+ HCP!

Wild? Dangerous? Bizarre? – yes, probably! Only 16 HCP to wade in with a 3NT bid and a balanced hand to boot? OK, your concerns are understandable, so I'll explain.

The preempter has between 6-10 HCP. You have 16 HCP. On an average day that will leave 16 HCP lurking in the unknown between the other two hands. If you chicken out of bidding and partner has only half of those points – and why not 9 or 10 HCP – you will have been conned out of your game when partner is unsuitable for protecting. It is, therefore, a calculated risk worth taking.

Your thoughts are misguided if you are now wondering why a double won't suffice on these balanced hands. Spare a thought for partner who may hold a reasonable hand without a stop in their suit.

EXAMPLE HANDS:
Right-hand opponent opens 3♡. Do you overcall?

♠ Q86	♠ KQJ765	♠ AQJ5	♠ KQ32	♠ AKJ8765
♡ KQ987	♡ 65	♡ 7	♡ AQ	♡ 52
◊ A43	◊ AK4	◊ KQ32	◊ KJ4	◊ A4
♣ 32	♣ J6	♣ A654	♣ J986	♣ A4
11 HCP	14 HCP	16 HCP	16 HCP	16 HCP
Pass	3♠	Double	3NT	4♠

EXAMPLE HANDS:
Left-hand opponent opens 3♣ passed round to you. Do you protect?

♠ QJ87	♠ 7	♠ AJ6	♠ A4	♠ AKJ87
♡ KQ76	♡ KQ975	♡ KQ65	♡ KQJ9876	♡ AKQ2
◊ A532	◊ AK765	◊ K6	◊ K83	◊ K765
♣ 6	♣ K4	♣ K987	♣ K	♣ -
12 HCP	15 HCP	16 HCP	16 HCP	20 HCP
Double	3♡	3NT	4♡	Double

In response to partner's action you will have to be sensitive to both the level at which you may be forced to reply plus the prevailing vulnerability. But, in any event, don't forget that you may need to jump the bidding to distinguish between a hand that has nothing (less than 8 HCP) and a hand that has something!

POINT TO PONDER

Bridge is all about out-scoring your opponents. After an opposing preempt, however, life can be difficult and you may have to settle for the best score possible rather than the best possible score!

Chapter 12

COPING WITH INTERVENTION

(A) HOW NATURAL BIDS ARE AFFECTED: PLUS THE PENALTY DOUBLE

The end of the book is in sight. But before you can be let loose against "those who are thirsty for your blood" – otherwise known as opponents – there's a bit more you need to know about competitive bidding.

Unfortunate though it is, interference can stem the normal flow of bidding quite dramatically. This chapter will show you the quirks you will have to contend with when your auction is disrupted by an overcaller.

Partner opens the bidding with 1♣ and you were about to respond 1◊ holding ...

        ♠ 843
        ♡ Q65
        ◊ K8762
        ♣ J3

... when RHO overcalls 1♠. What now? You were taught to respond with 6 HCP, but there is clearly no sensible bid at your disposal. Why? Because ...

> ### RULE
> ... you STILL need 9+ HCP to respond in a new suit at the two level

> ### RULE
> ... you cannot introduce No Trumps without a stop in the opponent's bid suit.

Quelle horreur! You must PASS!

While partner will be somewhat disappointed at your silence there is some light at the end of the tunnel. Partner WILL get another chance to speak.

Your predicament can be worse still when you are forced to pass with an even better hand! e.g.

♠ 65432
♡ AK2
◇ J87
♣ 32

However, please rest assured that it's not always doom and gloom in this department, though sometimes you will need to improvise.

HOT TIP

You should consider raising partner's suit with just 3-card support.

For example, partner opens the bidding with 1♡ and your RHO overcalls 2♣. You may not think so now, but a bid of 2♡ is a reasonable gamble when Pass is your only other choice holding ...

♠ AJ6
♡ K83
◇ 8542
♣ 532

... but I'm not going to twist your arm! Just don't complain to me when partner does not contest the auction further and you've missed a partscore.

Oh! and before I forget ...

RULE

A new major suit introduced at the two level promises at least five cards in that suit.

So, on the odd occasion you might be forced to introduce a new minor suit with only three cards, but it's unlikely to cause a disaster.

The *pièce de résistance* for responder is the enigmatic DOUBLE.

> ## RULE
>
> When partner's bid has shown points your double of an overcall is for PENALTY!

With as few as 9 HCP and a quality 4-card holding in the opponent's suit you can elect to double.

The auction opens with a 1♠ bid from partner followed by an overcall of 2◊. Your bid?;

♠ 82
♡ A54
◊ KQJ8
♣ J432

Double! Can you think of a better way to get a plus score? Of course this may not become the final contract, but for now you will have at least expressed the best feature of your hand.

You can also surprise an unsuspecting 1NT overcaller who may think he's immune with such a good hand! He will need more than 15-18 HCP to get himself out of this sandwich! With at least the balance of points between you, the opponents' lives will be a misery in 1NT doubled and probably any other contract to which they might attempt to escape.

If a double of a 1NT overcall shows 9+ HCP, a new suit at the two level is released to show a good 6-card suit with fewer points. It is to play, like a weak takeout but with a bit of ooomph!

Partner opens 1♡ and RHO overcalls 1NT.

(a) ♠ KQJ98   (b) ♠ KQJ987
     ♡ 2   ♡ 43
     ◊ A87   ◊ 543
     ♣ 7654   ♣ 32

Hand (a) clearly merits a double. With an attacking spade lead and a certain diamond entry things are looking rosy for the defence.

Hand (b) oozes playing strength, but is unlikely to be much use defensively. Bid 2♠.

Penalty doubles are lucrative and good fun (for your side), but they will not always solve your bidding problems. Neither are they always appropriate.

For example, partner opens 1♠ and RHO butts in with 2♦.

(c)		(d)	
	♠ Q3		♠ K54
	♡ KQ6		♡ AQ2
	♦ AJ42		♦ 5432
	♣ J654		♣ KJ6

Hand (c) has the values for 3NT and the healthy diamond stop required, so bid it! A penalty double is not as attractive with a relatively weak diamond holding and a game bonus looming.

Hand (d) should also be played in game, but you can hardly suggest No Trumps here. A bid of the opponent's suit comes to your aid again. It shows game points and primarily requests a stop in the enemy suit for 3NT, although any information that will direct the partnership to the best game contract will be gratefully received.

Intervention can certainly do strange things to poor responder, but can opener stay immune?

NO!

HOT TIP

Opener's rebid – when partner has not promised any points – needs extra values. Proceed with caution.

Let's say you open the bidding with 1♡, intending to rebid 1NT with your balanced 15 or 16 HCP. Instead of getting a peep out of partner the auction passes round to your RHO who 'protects' with 1♠. You can forget about your 1NT rebid now because facing a passed partner it now shows 17-19 HCP! Think of it as a safety net in case partner has nothing.

Varying the scenario slightly we'll let partner respond 1♠ this time. Just as you are about to rebid 1NT your RHO comes in with 2♣. Guess what? 2NT shows 17-18 HCP – because you are still responding to a hand which may have only 6 HCP.

You do have options available, not least of which is Pass; after all, partner will get another chance to bid. Double is also available – with the right shaped hand – but remember the golden rule for when it's takeout and when it's penalty.

EXAMPLE HANDS:
Partner opens 1♡. RHO overcalls 2♣. Your go.

♠ KQ3	♠ A4	♠ 8532	♠ QJ5	♠ AJ5
♡ J5	♡ K76	♡ 86	♡ 962	♡ Q32
◇ J543	◇ J7653	◇ AQ2	◇ KJ6	◇ AQ5
♣ 7654	♣ 432	♣ KQ98	♣ AQ32	♣ 7652
7 HCP	8 HCP	11 HCP	13 HCP	13 HCP
Pass!	2♡	Double	3NT	3♣!

EXAMPLE HANDS:
YOU open 1◇ passed round to RHO who 'protects' with 1♠. What do you bid?

♠ -	♠ 3	♠ K54	♠ AQJ	♠ A
♡ KQJ4	♡ A2	♡ QJ3	♡ K4	♡ AJ87
◇ A8752	◇ KQJ54	◇ KJ654	◇ AKQ2	◇ KQ54
♣ KJ54	♣ KQ876	♣ AJ	♣ 8763	♣ AJ54
14 HCP	15 HCP	15 HCP	19 HCP	19 HCP
Double	2♣	Pass	1NT!	Double

(B) RESPONDING TO PARTNER'S OPENING BID AFTER RHO HAS DOUBLED; PLUS THE REDOUBLE

When partner's opening bid is doubled by your RHO normal methods for responding occasionally benefit from some alternative thinking.

It is safe to assume that the doubler will hold hand-type (a) i.e. 11+ HCP with a shortage in the opening bid suit. Obviously hoping to find a fit at a sane level your opponents would now relish the space for exploration. Time to put on your bidding boots!

With support for partner you can certainly make life very difficult for them. Even without a fit you may still be able to thwart their plans. Better still, a juicy penalty may be in the offing.

In fact, following a double, you have a variety of disruptive manoeuvres at your disposal which are not normally on the menu without such an overcall.

(1) Holding less than 6 HCP you should still pass EXCEPT when you have support for partner's suit and at least 4 HCP.

1♡-(X)-Pass	♠ J65	♠ 654
	♡ 64	♡ J643
	◊ QJ6	◊ 986
	♣ 86432	♣ J54

(2) You may raise partner's suit to the two level with just 3 cards to an honour in support and 6-9 HCP. With a 4-card fit stick to the two level if your hand is balanced.

1♡-(X)-2♡	♠ K62	♠ Q4
	♡ Q653	♡ AJ6
	◊ J97	◊ 9862
	♣ 643	♣ J865

(3) With an increased range of 4-9 HCP and 4-card support you should preempt to the three level with a more shapely collection.

1♡-(X)-3♡	♠ 5	♠ 32
	♡ KJ76	♡ KQ87
	◊ 97642	◊ 65
	♣ 432	♣ J6542

(4) A supportive leap to the four level expresses an even greater distribution with 4-9 HCP and usually 5+ trumps.

1♡-(X)-4♡	♠ J83	♠ 43
	♡ AJ7652	♡ KJ765
	◊ 654	◊ 7
	♣ 2	♣ 98654

(5) Hope you can remember how to bid naturally!

1♡-(X)-1♠	♠ KQ87	♠ A8763
	♡ 642	♡ 72
	◇ Q87	◇ 43
	♣ 864	♣ QJ54

(6) On the grounds of frequency and necessity a jump shift should now be used to show a good 6-card suit and 6-9 HCP.

1♡-(X)-2♠	♠ KQJ765	♠ AQJ752
	♡ 54	♡ 2
	◇ 974	◇ J87
	♣ 32	♣ 542

(7) EXCEPT! If you are a passed hand your jump shift only promises a good 5-card suit but you MUST have four cards in partner's suit too and a near maximum for your initial pass.

1♡-(X)-2♠	♠ AQJ76	♠ KQ987
	♡ QJ32	♡ KJ65
	◇ 432	◇ 98
	♣ 3	♣ J5

(8) If raising partner immediately describes a weak hand how do you indicate a good hand with support? A 2NT bid normally shows a balanced hand with 10-12 HCP. After a double it takes on a completely different meaning. Use it to tell partner you have a minimum of 10 HCP with at least four of partner's suit.

1♡-(X)-2NT	♠ A3	♠ 987
	♡ AQ54	♡ KJ54
	◇ J864	◇ AK65
	♣ 543	♣ Q2

(9) The time has come to introduce you to the redouble. As a riposte to a double it cannot be employed at any other time. While it can have a variety of meanings the message here would convey a hand of 9+ HCP

with an almost identical shape to the doubler! Inferences strongly suggest that the opponents have unwittingly entered the auction at a dangerous time for them and a penalty may well be looming.

1♡-(X)-XX	♠ K654 ♡ 2 ◊ AJ76 ♣ QJ87	♠ QJ76 ♡ 87 ◊ KQ54 ♣ A43

EXAMPLE HANDS: 1♡ - (X) - ?

♠ J76 ♡ 9863 ◊ Q43 ♣ J64	♠ 76 ♡ KJ5 ◊ Q542 ♣ 7654	♠ AJ9 ♡ Q7 ◊ J765 ♣ 9876	♠ KQJ876 ♡ 6 ◊ Q87 ♣ J82	♠ K87 ♡ AQ87 ◊ 8543 ♣ Q2
4 HCP	6 HCP	8 HCP	9 HCP	11 HCP
Pass	2♡	1NT	2♠ *if not passed*	2NT

EXAMPLE HANDS: 1♠ - (X) - ?

♠ J876 ♡ 7 ◊ KJ653 ♣ 543	♠ KQ654 ♡ 3 ◊ Q6543 ♣ 73	♠ 87 ♡ AJ87 ◊ Q976 ♣ K76	♠ KQ32 ♡ 54 ◊ KQ875 ♣ J4	♠ J87 ♡ A2 ◊ Q2 ♣ KJ8763
5 HCP	7 HCP	10 HCP	11 HCP	11 HCP
3♠	4♠	Redouble	3◊ *if passed*	2♣

HOT TIP

Messing up the auction for your charming opponents can be fun but bear in mind they might know how to return the favour on another occasion. Keep your takeout doubles up to scratch and you'll live to tell another tale!

(C) COMPETITIVE BIDDING AFTER YOUR SIDE HAS OPENED INT

The INT opening bid is the centrepiece of the Acol system. Just as interference can cause havoc over a suit opening bid, interference here can be just as harmful.

Countermeasures for the responder are called for.

HERE ARE SOME OF YOUR OPTIONS AS RESPONDER TO THE INT OPENER WHEN YOUR RHO HAS OVERCALLED;

1. A bid of 2♣ is no longer Stayman when your RHO doubles INT. It is a weak takeout into clubs which, once in a while, will come in very handy!

2. If your hand is strong enough to go to game – i.e. 13+ HCP and you want to explore for a major-suit fit a bid of the OPPONENT'S suit replaces Stayman.

3. If INT is doubled responder can REDOUBLE to show 9+ HCP. This is a very expensive move for the opponents who have to decide whether to defend INT redoubled – which may prove impossible to beat – or escape into a contract of their own which will undoubtedly be doubled itself. Not for the faint-hearted!

4. When RHO overcalls with a suit bid you are free to compete in your suit at the two level if you wish. Your range is still 0-10 HCP but, as you were not forced to bid, it should be a genuine attempt to get a plus score.

5. Competing at the three level in your minor suit is INVITATIONAL with at least a 6-carder. Major suits promise GAME values and a 5-card suit.

6. 2NT still shows 11 or 12 HCP and game interest opposite a maximum, but should you have doubled instead?

7. DOUBLE IS PENALTY promising the usual 9+ HCP with a decent 4-card trump holding. As an added incentive remember partner has at least two of them as well!

EXAMPLE HANDS: 1NT - (X) - ?

♠ 98765	♠ 5432	♠ 63	♠ 75	♠ KJ7
♡ 432	♡ 875	♡ J6	♡ 97532	♡ Q98
◇ 32	◇ J73	◇ 983	◇ 32	◇ QJ96
♣ 543	♣ 543	♣ J87654	♣ QJ65	♣ J76
0 HCP	1 HCP	2 HCP	3 HCP	10 HCP
2♠	Pass	2♣!	2♡	Redouble

EXAMPLE HANDS: 1NT - (2♡) - ?

♠ K8765	♠ Q432	♠ AJ7	♠ KJ98	♠ AK973
♡ 42	♡ J2	♡ KQJ8	♡ A4	♡ 97
◇ K875	◇ AJ7	◇ 654	◇ 986	◇ Q87
♣ 97	♣ K652	♣ J82	♣ KQJ2	♣ AJ6
6 HCP	11 HCP	12 HCP	14 HCP	14 HCP
2♠	2NT	Double	3♡!	3♠

EXAMPLE HANDS: 1NT - (2♠) - ?

♠ 532	♠ K8765	♠ J86	♠ A3	♠ 876
♡ Q7	♡ 42	♡ 54	♡ KQJ98	♡ AQ6
◇ J5	◇ K875	◇ K8	◇ QJ6	◇ AJ642
♣ QJ7654	♣ 97	♣ AQJ654	♣ 87	♣ Q2
6 HCP	6 HCP	11 HCP	13 HCP	13 HCP
Pass	Pass!	3♣	3♡	3NT

I wish the content of this book contained everything you ever needed to know about Bridge. While some of the topics covered are minutely detailed others have only had their surface scratched.

But I can assure you that a comprehensive understanding of what you have just read will give you many happy hours playing the best card game ever!

QUIZ

Construct an auction for each pair of hands. Alternatively you can bid them with your favourite partner.

Hands 1-10: Dealer West.

1.

WEST	EAST
♠ A32	♠ KQ76
♡ AQ32	♡ KJ7
◇ 975	◇ K86
♣ A84	♣ 765

2.

WEST	EAST
♠ K9	♠ QJ73
♡ AQ65	♡ 932
◇ KQJ76	◇ A2
♣ J8	♣ K974

3.

WEST	EAST
♠ 7	♠ AQ65
♡ AK865	♡ QJ7
◇ A753	◇ KQ2
♣ Q54	♣ 972

4.

WEST	EAST
♠ J76	♠ KQ843
♡ K7	♡ 32
◇ AK753	◇ QJ6
♣ Q32	♣ AJ6

5.

WEST	EAST
♠ K9654	♠ AQ3
♡ 43	♡ 876
◇ A	◇ KQJ43
♣ AQ876	♣ J3

6.

	WEST	EAST
♠	KQ753	J4
♡	AQ54	J8
◇	A7	Q65432
♣	32	K87

7.

	WEST	EAST
♠	AJ97	K6
♡	K532	A8
◇	KQ87	J32
♣	K	QJ9876

8.

	WEST	EAST
♠	AKQ6	J1095
♡	5	KQ64
◇	K4	AJ3
♣	AK8765	Q4

9.

	WEST	EAST
♠	QJ76	AK98
♡	KQ43	A86
◇	J7	Q3
♣	KJ8	Q543

10.

	WEST	EAST
♠	A7654	KQ9
♡	QJ8	K76
◇	K8	432
♣	AK2	8765

Hands 11-20: Dealer East.

11.

	WEST	EAST
♠	Q743	5
♡	965	AK874
◇	J87	KQ2
♣	QJ7	AK92

	WEST	EAST
12.	♠ AJ98	♠ 43
	♡ KQ43	♡ J76
	◇ J52	◇ AK4
	♣ J4	♣ KQ876
13.	WEST	EAST
	♠ 6543	♠ AQ8
	♡ A97	♡ KQ2
	◇ KQJ	◇ A752
	♣ J43	♣ KQ7
14.	WEST	EAST
	♠ Q65	♠ K8
	♡ K84	♡ J65
	◇ K432	◇ AQJ765
	♣ QJ3	♣ K4
15.	WEST	EAST
	♠ 2	♠ AQJ54
	♡ QJ64	♡ K975
	◇ AK87	◇ Q2
	♣ A432	♣ 98
16.	WEST	EAST
	♠ KJ53	♠ 4
	♡ Q43	♡ KJ765
	◇ 6432	◇ A95
	♣ 86	♣ AKQ5
17.	WEST	EAST
	♠ AJ43	♠ K82
	♡ QJ43	♡ K87
	◇ J87	◇ AQ3
	♣ 32	♣ QJ76

18.

	WEST	EAST
♠	4	AKJ82
♡	Q983	J6
◇	J973	KQ2
♣	J876	AKQ

19.

	WEST	EAST
♠	KQ32	AJ865
♡	Q543	AKJ
◇	A65	2
♣	97	KQJ5

20.

	WEST	EAST
♠	54	KJ87
♡	76	AQ32
◇	QJ654	K8
♣	QJ43	K76

Hands 21-30: Dealer South, who opens 1♡.
No further bidding by North/South.

21.

	WEST	EAST
♠	J3	A98
♡	Q63	K5
◇	A7	K6543
♣	KJ9865	A72

22.

	WEST	EAST
♠	KQ32	8765
♡	4	832
◇	AK92	J73
♣	Q532	J84

23.

	WEST	EAST
♠	AQ986	KJ3
♡	K54	76
◇	A52	KQJ3
♣	54	J863

	WEST	EAST
24.		
	♠ KQ6	♠ A852
	♡ QJ9876	♡ 3
	◊ A2	◊ K973
	♣ 654	♣ A982
25.	WEST	EAST
	♠ AKQJ76	♠ 2
	♡ A2	♡ J654
	◊ 53	◊ KQ76
	♣ J52	♣ 8643
26.	WEST	EAST
	♠ AQ54	♠ K987
	♡ AQ87	♡ J42
	◊ Q32	◊ A754
	♣ 32	♣ A7
27.	WEST	EAST
	♠ AJ5	♠ 973
	♡ AJ8	♡ Q2
	◊ K8	◊ Q9765
	♣ AQJ93	♣ K62
28.	WEST	EAST
	♠ AK987654	♠ 3
	♡ 54	♡ 9872
	◊ A	◊ 6543
	♣ Q2	♣ K765
29.	WEST	EAST
	♠ KJ84	♠ 32
	♡ 86	♡ K92
	◊ AK65	◊ Q82
	♣ KQ7	♣ AJ854

30.   WEST   EAST
        ♠ Q43   ♠ J6
        ♡ AJ63   ♡ 72
        ◇ K9   ◇ Q87652
        ♣ AQ32   ♣ J76

Hands 31-40: Dealer West. North overcalls 2♡.
No further bidding by North/South.

31.   WEST   EAST
        ♠ A82   ♠ K2
        ♡ 98   ♡ KQ76
        ◇ J8642   ◇ 753
        ♣ AQJ   ♣ K872

32.   WEST   EAST
        ♠ QJ987   ♠ K54
        ♡ K4   ♡ Q32
        ◇ KQJ65   ◇ 32
        ♣ 4   ♣ K8765

33.   WEST   EAST
        ♠ QJ6   ♠ AK743
        ♡ 43   ♡ J5
        ◇ K6   ◇ Q53
        ♣ AQJ876   ♣ K93

34.   WEST   EAST
        ♠ KQJ86   ♠ 32
        ♡ 5   ♡ AQ98
        ◇ AK92   ◇ J75
        ♣ 432   ♣ KJ97

35.   WEST   EAST
        ♠ K865   ♠ AQJ4
        ♡ AK3   ♡ 87
        ◇ Q765   ◇ AKJ4
        ♣ J8   ♣ 432

36.

WEST	EAST
♠ A986	♠ K43
♡ AQ3	♡ 876
◇ J76	◇ AKQ2
♣ KJ3	♣ Q42

37.

WEST	EAST
♠ J3	♠ AK7
♡ Q87	♡ J54
◇ KJ654	◇ AQ3
♣ AQ7	♣ 6543

38.

WEST	EAST
♠ 3	♠ KJ65
♡ KQ	♡ 743
◇ AJ6543	◇ Q987
♣ Q843	♣ KJ

39.

WEST	EAST
♠ KQ5	♠ AJ876
♡ K982	♡ A3
◇ 76	◇ 32
♣ A543	♣ KJ62

40.

WEST	EAST
♣ 9876	♣ AJ3
♡ AQ7	♡ 32
◇ A32	◇ 54
♣ KJ2	♣ AQ9876

Hands 41-50: Dealer East. South doubles.
No further bidding by North/South.

41.

WEST	EAST
♠ Q543	♠ KJ876
♡ 6	♡ KQ2
◇ J5432	◇ A876
♣ K63	♣ Q

42.   WEST   EAST

           ♠ 765   ♠ A
           ♡ KJ32   ♡ A87654
           ◇ J7   ◇ KQ32
           ♣ AQ86   ♣ J4

43.   WEST   EAST

           ♠ KJ54   ♠ 87
           ♡ QJ54   ♡ K2
           ◇ Q543   ◇ K6
           ♣ 3   ♣ KQ87654

44.   WEST   EAST

           ♠ 2   ♠ J65
           ♡ K9843   ♡ AJ752
           ◇ 53   ◇ 4
           ♣ K8432   ♣ AQ75

45.   WEST   EAST

           ♠ Q642   ♠ AK83
           ♡ J92   ♡ Q54
           ◇ K43   ◇ Q2
           ♣ Q86   ♣ KJ97

46.   WEST   EAST

           ♠ J43   ♠ KQ76
           ♡ Q86   ♡ J4
           ◇ Q97   ◇ K8642
           ♣ K843   ♣ AJ

47.   WEST   EAST

           ♠ 653   ♠ AQ4
           ♡ K6543   ♡ 98
           ◇ J32   ◇ KQ65
           ♣ 65   ♣ J973

48.	WEST	EAST
	♠ 32	♠ KQ54
	♡ 94	♡ QJ8765
	◊ A32	◊ K7
	♣ AJ8765	♣ 2
49.	WEST	EAST
	♠ 832	♠ J76
	♡ AQJ987	♡ 5
	◊ 43	◊ AJ76
	♣ 32	♣ KQJ54
50.	WEST	EAST
	♠ KJ92	♠ Q8765
	♡ Q2	♡ KJ76
	◊ KJ54	◊ A2
	♣ J87	♣ Q4

Hands 51-60: Dealer West.

51.	WEST	EAST
	♠ A54	♠ KQJ876
	♡ KQJ87	♡ A3
	◊ KJ6	◊ A8
	♣ 43	♣ K87
52.	WEST	EAST
	♠ A72	♠ KQ
	♡ KJ54	♡ AQ8
	◊ A86	◊ KQJ2
	♣ Q43	♣ K987
53.	WEST	EAST
	♠ 32	♠ AQ7
	♡ AK876	♡ 43
	◊ AKQ3	◊ J76
	♣ 32	♣ KQ765

54.

WEST	EAST
♠ KQ654	♠ 32
♡ Q7	♡ KJ54
◇ KQ87	◇ 32
♣ K8	♣ AQJ54

55.

WEST	EAST
♠ AKQ65	♠ J7
♡ AKJ87	♡ Q65
◇ A3	◇ 76542
♣ 5	♣ 987

56.

WEST	EAST
♠ 42	♠ A3
♡ 965	♡ 83
◇ 6	◇ AK987
♣ KQJ8765	♣ A932

57.

WEST	EAST
♠ AK8742	♠ QJ96
♡ J43	♡ 765
◇ KQJ	◇ A98
♣ A	♣ KJ7

58.

WEST	EAST
♠ KQ4	♠ AJ7
♡ K973	♡ A4
◇ QJ62	◇ K98
♣ A6	♣ KQJ43

59.

WEST	EAST
♠ 76	♠ K932
♡ AQJ765	♡ K982
◇ AKQ	◇ 65
♣ A3	♣ 876

60.   WEST   EAST

        ♠ KQJ   ♠ 543
        ♡ KQ43   ♡ A876
        ◇ AQ3   ◇ K98
        ♣ Q54   ♣ J62

ANSWERS:

(opponents calls are in brackets)
* artificial bids are asterisked

1.   1NT-2NT-3NT

2.   1◇-1♠-2♡-3NT

3.   1♡-1♠-2◇-4♡

4.   1NT-3♠-4♠

5.   1♣-1◇-1♠-2♡*-2♠-4♠

6.   1♠-1NT-2♡-2♠-Pass

7.   1♡-2♣-2NT-3NT

8.   1♣-1♡-2♠-3♠-4NT*-5◇*-6♠

9.   1NT-2♣*-2♡-3NT-4♠

10. 1♠-1NT-2NT-3♣-4♠

11. 1♡-1♠-3♣-4♡

12. 1NT-2♣*-2◇*-2NT-3NT

13. 2NT-4NT-Pass

14. 1◇-3◇-3NT or 1◇-2NT-3NT

15. 1♠-2♣-2♡-4♡

16. 1♡-1♠-2♣-2♡-2NT-3♡-Pass

17. 1♣-1♡-1NT-2NT-Pass

18. 2♣*-2◊*-2NT-3♣*-3♠-3NT

19. 1♠-3♠-4NT*-5◊*-6♠

20. 1♡-1NT-Pass

21. (1♡)-2♣-3NT

22. (1♡)-X-1♠-Pass

23. (1♡)-1♠-3♠-4♠

24. (1♡)-Pass-X-Pass

25. (1♡)-2♠-Pass

26. (1♡)-Pass-1NT-2♣*-2♠-4♠

27. (1♡)-X-2◊-2NT-3NT

28. (1♡)-4♠-Pass

29. (1♡)-X-3♣-3♡*-3NT

30. (1♡)-1NT-2◊-Pass

31. 1NT-(2♡)-X-Pass

32. 1♠-(2♡)-2♠-Pass

33. 1♣-(2♡)-2♠-3♠-4♠

34. 1♠-(2♡)-X

35. 1NT-(2♡)-3♡*-3♠-4♠

36. 1♠-(2♡)-3♡*-3NT-Pass

37. 1NT-(2♡)-3NT

38. 1◊-(2♡)-3◊-Pass

39. 1NT-(2♡)-3♠-4♠

40. 1NT-(2♡)-3♣-3NT

41. 1♠-(X)-3♠-Pass

42. 1♡-(X)-2NT*-4♡

43. 1♣-(X)-XX-2♣-Pass

44. 1♡-(X)-4♡

45. 1♠-(X)-2♠-Pass

46. 1◇-(X)-1NT-Pass

47. 1NT-(X)-2♡-Pass

48. 1♡-(X)-2♣-2♡-Pass

49. 1♣-(X)-2♡-Pass

50. 1♠-(X)-2NT*-3♠-Pass

51. 1♡-2♠-3♣-4NT*-5◇*-6♠

52. 1NT-4NT-6NT

53. 1♡-2♣-3◇-3NT

54. 1♠-2♣-2◇-2NT-3NT

55. 2♠-2NT*-3♡-3♠-4♡-Pass

56. 3♣-5♣

57. 1♠-3♠-4♣*-4◇*-4♠-Pass

58. 1♡-3♣-3NT-6NT

59. 2♡-4♡-Pass

60. 1♡-2♡-3NT-Pass

GLOSSARY OF TERMS

ACOL
A bidding system that is standard in Britain and widely played in other parts of the world.

ARTIFICIAL
An unnatural call that does not promise the suit mentioned – like 2♣ over 1NT for Stayman.

BALANCED
A hand pattern which has no singleton, no void, and not more than one doubleton.

BARRIER
An imaginary concept to aid reverse bidding. The barrier is two of the suit that has been opened.

BONUS
A premium score for bidding and making a game or slam.

CONVENTIONAL
A call with a defined meaning which may be artificial with no significance to the suit named.

DISTRIBUTIONAL POINTS
Used to grade a hand with suits of extra length or shortages that are useful on the auction.

DOUBLE JUMP OVERCALL
Competing with a jump bid which misses out two levels of bidding.

DOUBLETON
A suit of only two cards.

FORCING
A bid that cannot be passed.

GAME
3NT, 4♡, 4♠, 5♣ or 5♢; a contract bid at a level which scores at least 100 trick score points.

GAME-FORCING
A bid which commits the partnership to game.

GRAND SLAM
A contract bid at the seven level; 7♣, 7♢, 7♡, 7♠, 7NT.

HCP = HIGH CARD POINTS
Ace = 4 HCP; King = 3 HCP; Queen = 2 HCP; Jack = 1 HCP.

HONOUR CARDS
Ace; King; Queen; Jack; Ten.

INVITATIONAL
A bid which encourages the partner to continue to a game or slam.

JUMP PREFERENCE
Choosing one of partner's suits with a jump bid.

JUMP SHIFT
A new suit introduced with a jump bid.

LHO
Left-hand opponent.

LIMIT BID
A bid which defines a limited point range. May be weak or strong.

MAJOR SUIT
Hearts or spades.

MINOR SUIT
Clubs or diamonds.

NATURAL
As it sounds – not conventional or artificial!

NEGATIVE RESPONSE
A conventional and artificial response to a forcing opening bid to show a weak hand in context.

NEGATIVE CONTROL
Singleton or void.

NON-FORCING
A bid which can be passed.

NONVULNERABLE
A side which is yet to win a game.

ONE-ROUND FORCE
This bid cannot be passed.

OVERCALL
A competitive bid after an opponent has opened the auction.

PARTSCORE
A contract which attracts less than 100 trick score points.

PENALTY
Points awarded to the defenders when declarer's contract fails.

POSITIVE RESPONSE
A conventional but natural response to a forcing opening bid to show a strong hand in context.

POSITIVE CONTROL
Ace or King.

PREEMPTIVE
An obstructive call which takes up an unusual amount of bidding space.

PRIMARY SUPPORT
Able to support partner's suit to make an 8-card fit.

RANK
In ascending order = clubs; diamonds; hearts; spades; No Trumps.

REVERSE
A rebid by opener in a new suit above the barrier.

RHO
Right-hand opponent.

SEMI-BALANCED
A hand pattern that has more than one doubleton, but no void or singleton.

SHORTAGE
Two or fewer cards in a suit.

SIGN OFF
Expressing a wish to name the final contract it is a command for partner to pass.

SIMPLE OVERCALL
Competing without jumping the bidding.

SIMPLE PREFERENCE
Choosing one of partner's suits without jumping the bidding.

SIMPLE RESPONSE
Responding to partner without jumping the bidding.

SINGLE JUMP OVERCALL
Competing with a jump bid that only misses one level of bidding.

SINGLETON
Only one card in a suit.

SMALL SLAM
A contract bid at the six level; 6♣, 6◊, 6♡, 6♠, 6NT.

STOP or STOPPER
A combination of high cards in one suit that hopes to produce at least one trick if this suit is lead by the defenders.

STRAIN
A term encompassing all suits or No Trumps.

UNBALANCED
A hand pattern which contain either a singleton or a void.

UNLIMITED
A bid which defines an unlimited point range.

VOID
No cards in a suit.

VULNERABLE
A term applied to a side which has won a game, thus attracting greater penalties or premiums.

X; DOUBLE
As a penalty it increases the scoring value of a contract made or its undertricks; also used conventionally to ask partner to pick the trump suit.

XX; REDOUBLE
Can only be used following a double to increase the score yet again; can also be used conventionally.

OTHER TERMINOLOGY

| 12+ | = | 12 or more |
| 12-19 | = | inclusive of 12 and 19 |

CONVENTIONS MENTIONED IN THIS BOOK

BLACKWOOD
A bid of 4NT, when not deemed to be natural, is an aid to slam bidding to check for Aces and Kings.

CUE BID
A bid of a suit above 3NT, other than the agreed trump suit, shows a positive or negative control in the suit bid and interest in a slam.

FOURTH-SUIT FORCING
A bid of the fourth suit in an unopposed auction is conventional, requesting further information.

GERBER
A convention used to ask for Aces directly after partner has opened 1NT or 2NT, as a substitute for Blackwood.

STAYMAN
A 2♣ call is used to locate a major suit fit over a 1NT opening bid; a 1NT overcall; or a protective 1NT overcall.